Global Investment Performance Standards

2010

As adopted by the GIPS® Executive
Committee on 29 January 2010

ISBN: 978-0-938367-98-7
December 2014

CONTENTS

PREFACE

CFA Institute is a global not-for-profit association of investment professionals with the mission of leading the investment profession globally by setting the highest standards of ethics, education, and professional excellence. CFA Institute has a long-standing history of and commitment to establishing a broadly accepted ethical standard for calculating and presenting investment performance based on the principles of fair representation and full disclosure. The goals in developing and evolving the Global Investment Performance Standards (GIPS) are to establish them as the recognized standard for calculating and presenting investment performance around the world and for the GIPS standards to become a firm's "passport" to market investment management services globally. As of January 2010, CFA Institute has partnered with organizations in 32 countries that contribute to the development and promotion of the GIPS standards.

History

In 1995, CFA Institute, formerly known as the Association for Investment Management and Research (AIMR), sponsored and funded the Global Investment Performance Standards Committee to develop global standards for calculating and presenting investment performance, based on the existing AIMR Performance Presentation Standards (AIMR-PPS®).

In 1998, the proposed GIPS standards were posted on the CFA Institute website and circulated for comment to more than 4,000 individuals who had expressed interest. The result was the first Global Investment Performance Standards, published in April 1999.

The initial edition of the GIPS standards was designed to create a minimum global investment performance standard that would:

- Permit and facilitate acceptance and adoption in developing markets;
- Give the global investment management industry one commonly accepted approach for calculating and presenting performance; and
- Address liquid asset classes (equity, fixed income, and cash).

In 1999, the Global Investment Performance Standards Committee was replaced by the Investment Performance Council (IPC) to further develop and promote the GIPS standards. The development of the GIPS standards was a global industry initiative with participation from individuals and organizations from more than 15 countries.

The IPC was charged with developing provisions for other asset classes (e.g., real estate, private equity) and addressing other performance-related issues (e.g., fees, advertising) to broaden the scope and applicability of the GIPS standards. This was accomplished when the second edition of the GIPS standards was published in February 2005.

With the release of the 2005 edition of the GIPS standards and growing adoption and expansion of the GIPS standards, the IPC decided to move to a single global investment performance standard and eliminate the need for local variations of the GIPS standards. All country-specific performance standards converged with the GIPS standards, resulting in 25 countries adopting a single, global standard for the calculation and presentation of investment performance.

In 2005, with the convergence of country-specific versions to the GIPS standards and the need to reorganize the governance structure to facilitate involvement from GIPS country sponsors, CFA Institute dissolved the IPC and created the GIPS Executive Committee and the GIPS Council. The GIPS Executive Committee serves as the decision-making authority for the GIPS standards, and the GIPS Council facilitates the involvement of all country sponsors in the ongoing development and promotion of the GIPS standards.

To maintain global relevance, and in recognition of the dynamic nature of the investment industry, the GIPS standards must be continually updated through interpretations, guidance, and new provisions. In 2008, the GIPS Executive Committee began its review of the GIPS standards in an effort to further refine the provisions as well as eliminate provisions that are no longer necessary and add new requirements and recommendations that promote best practice. The GIPS Executive Committee worked in close collaboration with its technical subcommittees, specially formed working groups, and GIPS country sponsors. These groups reviewed the existing provisions and guidance and conducted surveys and other research as part of the efforts to produce the 2010 edition of the GIPS standards.

INTRODUCTION

Preamble—Why Is a Global Investment Performance Standard Needed?

Standardized Investment Performance

Financial markets and the investment management industry have become increasingly global in nature. The growth in the types and number of financial entities, the globalization of the investment process, and the increased competition among investment management firms demonstrate the need to standardize the calculation and presentation of investment performance.

Global Passport

Asset managers and both existing and prospective clients benefit from an established global standard for calculating and presenting investment performance. Investment practices, regulation, performance measurement, and reporting of performance vary considerably from country to country. By adhering to a global standard, firms in countries with minimal or no investment performance standards will be able to compete for business on an equal footing with firms from countries with more developed standards. Firms from countries with established practices will have more confidence in being fairly compared with local firms when competing for business in countries that have not previously adopted performance standards. Performance standards that are accepted globally enable investment firms to measure and present their investment performance so that investors can readily compare investment performance among firms.

Investor Confidence

Investment managers that adhere to investment performance standards help assure investors that the firm's investment performance is complete and fairly presented. Both prospective and existing clients of investment firms benefit from a global investment performance standard by having a greater degree of confidence in the performance information presented to them.

Objectives

The establishment of a voluntary global investment performance standard leads to an accepted set of best practices for calculating and presenting investment performance that is readily comparable among investment firms, regardless of geographic location. These standards also facilitate a dialogue between investment firms and their existing and prospective clients regarding investment performance.

The goals of the GIPS Executive Committee are:

- To establish investment industry best practices for calculating and presenting investment performance that promote investor interests and instill investor confidence;
- To obtain worldwide acceptance of a single standard for the calculation and presentation of investment performance based on the principles of fair representation and full disclosure;
- To promote the use of accurate and consistent investment performance data;
- To encourage fair, global competition among investment firms without creating barriers to entry; and
- To foster the notion of industry "self-regulation" on a global basis.

Overview

Key features of the GIPS standards include the following:

- The GIPS standards are ethical standards for investment performance presentation to ensure fair representation and full disclosure of investment performance. In order to claim compliance, firms must adhere to the requirements included in the GIPS standards.
- Meeting the objectives of fair representation and full disclosure is likely to require more than simply adhering to the minimum requirements of the GIPS standards. Firms should also adhere to the recommendations to achieve best practice in the calculation and presentation of performance.

- The GIPS standards require firms to include all actual, discretionary, fee-paying portfolios in at least one composite defined by investment mandate, objective, or strategy in order to prevent firms from cherry-picking their best performance.

- The GIPS standards rely on the integrity of input data. The accuracy of input data is critical to the accuracy of the performance presentation. The underlying valuations of portfolio holdings drive the portfolio's performance. It is essential for these and other inputs to be accurate. The GIPS standards require firms to adhere to certain calculation methodologies and to make specific disclosures along with the firm's performance.

- Firms must comply with all requirements of the GIPS standards, including any updates, Guidance Statements, interpretations, Questions & Answers (Q&As), and clarifications published by CFA Institute and the GIPS Executive Committee, which are available on the GIPS website (www.gipsstandards.org) as well as in the *GIPS Handbook*.

The GIPS standards do not address every aspect of performance measurement or cover unique characteristics of each asset class. The GIPS standards will continue to evolve over time to address additional areas of investment performance. Understanding and interpreting investment performance requires consideration of both risk and return. Historically, the GIPS standards focused primarily on returns. In the spirit of fair representation and full disclosure, and in order to provide investors with a more comprehensive view of a firm's performance, the 2010 edition of the GIPS standards includes new provisions related to risk.

Historical Performance Record

- A firm is required to initially present, at a minimum, five years of annual investment performance that is compliant with the GIPS standards. If the firm or the composite has been in existence less than five years, the firm must present performance since the firm's inception or the composite inception date.

- After a firm presents a minimum of five years of GIPS-compliant performance (or for the period since the firm's inception or the composite inception date if the firm or the composite has been in existence less than five years), the firm must present an additional year of performance each year, building up to a minimum of 10 years of GIPS-compliant performance.

- Firms may link non-GIPS-compliant performance to their GIPS-compliant performance provided that only GIPS-compliant performance is presented for periods after 1 January 2000 and the firm discloses the periods of non-compliance. Firms must not link non-GIPS-compliant performance for periods beginning on or after 1 January 2000 to their GIPS-compliant performance. Firms that manage private equity, real estate, and/or wrap fee/separately managed account (SMA) portfolios must also comply with Sections 6, 7, and 8, respectively, of the Provisions of the GIPS standards that became effective as of 1 January 2006.

Compliance

Firms must take all steps necessary to ensure that they have satisfied all the requirements of the GIPS standards before claiming compliance. Firms are strongly encouraged to perform periodic internal compliance checks. Implementing adequate internal controls during all stages of the investment performance process—from data input to preparing performance presentations—will instill confidence in the validity of performance presented as well as in the claim of compliance.

Firms may choose to have an independent third-party verification that tests the construction of the firm's composites as well as the firm's policies and procedures as they relate to compliance with the GIPS standards. The value of verification is widely recognized, and being verified is considered to be best practice. The GIPS Executive Committee strongly recommends that firms be verified. In addition to verification, firms may also choose to have specifically focused composite testing (performance examination) performed by an independent third-party verifier to provide additional assurance regarding a particular composite.

Effective Date

The effective date for the 2010 edition of the GIPS standards is 1 January 2011. Compliant presentations that include performance for periods that begin on or after 1 January 2011 must be prepared in accordance with the 2010 edition of the GIPS standards. Prior editions of the GIPS standards may be found on the GIPS website (www.gipsstandards.org).

Implementing a Global Standard

The presence of a local sponsoring organization for investment performance standards is essential for effective implementation and ongoing support of the GIPS standards within a country. Such country sponsors also provide an important link between the GIPS Executive Committee, the governing body for the GIPS standards, and the local markets in which investment managers operate.

The country sponsor, by actively supporting the GIPS standards and the work of the GIPS Executive Committee, ensures that the country's interests are taken into account as the GIPS standards are developed. Compliance with the GIPS standards is voluntary, and support from the local country sponsor helps to drive the adoption of the GIPS standards.

The GIPS Executive Committee strongly encourages countries without an investment performance standard to promote the GIPS standards as the local standard and translate them into the local language when necessary. Although the GIPS standards may be translated into many languages, if a discrepancy arises, the English version of the GIPS standards is the official governing version.

The GIPS Executive Committee will continue to promote the principles of fair representation and full disclosure and develop the GIPS standards so that they maintain their relevance within the changing investment management industry.

The self-regulatory nature of the GIPS standards necessitates a strong commitment to ethical integrity. Self-regulation also assists regulators in exercising their responsibility for ensuring the fair disclosure of information within financial markets. The GIPS Executive Committee encourages regulators to:

- Recognize the benefit of voluntary compliance with standards that represent global best practices;
- Give consideration to taking enforcement actions against firms that falsely claim compliance with the GIPS standards; and
- Recognize and encourage independent third-party verification.

Where existing laws, regulations, or industry standards already impose requirements related to the calculation and presentation of investment performance, firms are strongly encouraged to comply with the GIPS standards in addition to applicable regulatory requirements. Compliance with applicable law and/or regulation does not necessarily lead to compliance with the GIPS standards. In cases in which laws and/or regulations conflict with the GIPS standards, firms are required to comply with the laws and regulations and make full disclosure of the conflict in the compliant presentation.

Country Sponsors

The presence of a local sponsoring organization for investment performance standards, known as a "country sponsor," is essential for effective implementation of the GIPS standards and ongoing support within a country. Country sponsors collectively form the GIPS Council, which provides a formal role in the ongoing development and oversight of the GIPS standards. Country sponsors:

- Promote the GIPS standards locally;
- Provide local market support and input for the GIPS standards;
- Present country-specific issues to the GIPS Executive Committee; and
- Participate in the governance of the GIPS standards via membership in the GIPS Council and Regional Investment Performance Subcommittees.

Each organization undergoes a formal review before being endorsed as a country sponsor. Additional information and a current list of country sponsors can be found on the GIPS website (www.gipsstandards.org).

Endorsed GIPS Country Sponsors (as of 1 January 2010)

Australia	Investment and Financial Services Association Limited—Performance Analyst Group
Austria	1) Österreichische Vereinigung für Finanzanalyse und Asset Management and 2) Vereinigung Österreichischer Investmentgesellschaften
Belgium	Belgian Asset Managers Association
Canada	Canadian Investment Performance Committee
Denmark	The Danish Society of Financial Analysts and CFA Denmark
France	1) Société Française des Analystes Financiers and 2) Association Française de la Gestion Financière
Germany	German Asset Management Standards Committee: 1) Bundesverband Investment und Asset Management e.V., 2) Deutsche Vereinigung für Finanzanalyse und Asset Management, and 3) German CFA Society
Greece	Hellenic CFA Society
Hong Kong	Local Sponsor: The Hong Kong Society of Financial Analysts
Hungary	1) CFA Society of Hungary and 2) the Association of Hungarian Investment Fund and Asset Management Companies
Ireland	Irish Association of Investment Managers
Italy	Italian Investment Performance Committee: 1) L'Associazione Bancaria Italiana, 2) L'Associazione Italiana degli Analisti Finanziari, 3) Assogestioni, 4) Sviluppo Mercato Fondi Pensione, 5) Assirevi, and 6) Italian CFA Society
Japan	The Security Analysts Association of Japan
Kazakhstan	Kazakhstan Association of Financial and Investment Analysts
Liechtenstein	Liechtenstein Bankers' Association
Micronesia	Asia Pacific Association for Fiduciary Studies
The Netherlands	The Netherlands Beroepsvereniging van Beleggingsprofessionals
New Zealand	CFA Society of New Zealand
Norway	The Norwegian Society of Financial Analysts
Pakistan	CFA Association of Pakistan
Portugal	Associação Portuguesa de Analista Financeiros
Russia	National League of Management Companies
Singapore	Investment Management Association of Singapore
South Africa	Association for Savings and Investment, South Africa
South Korea	Korea GIPS Committee
Spain	Asociación Española de Presentación de Resultados de Gestión
Sri Lanka	CFA Sri Lanka
Sweden	Swedish Society of Financial Analysts
Switzerland	Swiss Bankers Association
Ukraine	The Ukrainian Association of Investment Business
United Kingdom	UK Investment Performance Committee: 1) Association of British Insurers, 2) Investment Management Association, and 3) National Association of Pension Funds
United States	CFA Institute—US Investment Performance Committee

I. PROVISIONS OF THE GLOBAL INVESTMENT PERFORMANCE STANDARDS

The provisions within the GIPS standards are divided into the following nine sections: Fundamentals of Compliance, Input Data, Calculation Methodology, Composite Construction, Disclosure, Presentation and Reporting, Real Estate, Private Equity, and Wrap Fee/Separately Managed Account (SMA) Portfolios.

The provisions for each section are categorized into requirements and recommendations. Firms must meet all the requirements to claim compliance with the GIPS standards. Firms are encouraged to implement as many of the recommendations as possible. These recommended provisions are considered to be industry best practice and assist firms in fully adhering to the spirit and intent of the GIPS standards.

0   **Fundamentals of Compliance:** Several core principles create the foundation for the GIPS standards, including properly defining the firm, providing compliant presentations to all prospective clients, adhering to applicable laws and regulations, and ensuring that information presented is not false or misleading. Two important issues that a firm must consider when becoming compliant with the GIPS standards are the definition of the firm and the firm's definition of discretion. The definition of the firm is the foundation for firm-wide compliance and creates defined boundaries whereby total firm assets can be determined. The firm's definition of discretion establishes criteria to judge which portfolios must be included in a composite and is based on the firm's ability to implement its investment strategy.

1   **Input Data:** Consistency of input data used to calculate performance is critical to effective compliance with the GIPS standards and establishes the foundation for full, fair, and comparable investment performance presentations. For periods beginning on or after 1 January 2011, all portfolios must be valued in accordance with the definition of fair value and the GIPS Valuation Principles.

2   **Calculation Methodology:** Achieving comparability among investment management firms' performance presentations requires uniformity in methods used to calculate returns. The GIPS standards mandate the use of certain calculation methodologies to facilitate comparability.

3   **Composite Construction:** A composite is an aggregation of one or more portfolios managed according to a similar investment mandate, objective, or strategy. The composite return is the asset-weighted average of the performance of all portfolios in the composite. Creating meaningful composites is essential to the fair presentation, consistency, and comparability of performance over time and among firms.

4   **Disclosure:** Disclosures allow firms to elaborate on the data provided in the presentation and give the reader the proper context in which to understand the performance. To comply with the GIPS standards, firms must disclose certain information in all compliant presentations regarding their performance and the policies adopted by the firm. Although some disclosures are required for all firms, others are specific to certain circumstances and may not be applicable in all situations. Firms are not required to make negative assurance disclosures (e.g., if the firm does not use leverage in a particular composite strategy, no disclosure of the use of leverage is required). One of the essential disclosures for every firm is the claim of compliance. Once a firm meets all the requirements of the GIPS standards, it must appropriately use the claim of compliance to indicate compliance with the GIPS standards. The 2010 edition of the GIPS standards includes a revised compliance statement that indicates if the firm has or has not been verified.

5   **Presentation and Reporting:** After constructing the composites, gathering the input data, calculating returns, and determining the necessary disclosures, the firm must incorporate this information in presentations based on the requirements in the GIPS standards for presenting investment performance. No finite set of requirements can cover all potential situations or anticipate future developments in investment industry structure, technology, products, or practices. When appropriate, firms have the responsibility to include in GIPS-compliant presentations information not addressed by the GIPS standards.

6   **Real Estate:** Unless otherwise noted, this section supplements all of the required and recommended provisions in Sections 0–5. Real estate provisions were first included in the 2005 edition of the GIPS standards and became effective 1 January 2006. The 2010 edition of the GIPS standards includes new provisions for closed-end real estate funds. Firms should note that certain provisions of Sections 0–5 do not apply to real estate investments or are superseded by provisions within Section 6. The provisions that do not apply have been noted within Section 6.

7   **Private Equity:** Unless otherwise noted, this section supplements all of the required and recommended provisions in Sections 0–5. Private equity provisions were first included in the 2005 edition of the GIPS standards and became effective 1 January 2006. Firms should note that certain provisions in Sections 0–5 do not apply to private equity investments or are superseded by provisions within Section 7. The provisions that do not apply have been noted within Section 7.

8   **Wrap Fee/Separately Managed Account (SMA) Portfolios:** Unless otherwise noted, this section supplements all of the required and recommended provisions in Sections 0–5. Firms should note that certain provisions in Sections 0–5 of the GIPS standards do not apply to wrap fee/SMA portfolios or are superseded by provisions within Section 8. The provisions that do not apply have been noted within Section 8.

Defined Terms: Words appearing in small capital letters in the GIPS standards are defined in the GIPS **Glossary**, which is located at the end of this reading.

0 Fundamentals of Compliance

Fundamentals of Compliance—Requirements

0.A.1   FIRMS MUST comply with all the REQUIREMENTS of the GIPS standards, including any updates, Guidance Statements, interpretations, Questions & Answers (Q&As), and clarifications published by CFA Institute and the GIPS Executive Committee, which are available on the GIPS standards website (www.gipsstandards.org) as well as in the *GIPS Handbook.*

0.A.2   FIRMS MUST comply with all applicable laws and regulations regarding the calculation and presentation of performance.

0.A.3   FIRMS MUST NOT present performance or performance-related information that is false or misleading.

0.A.4   The GIPS standards MUST be applied on a FIRM-wide basis.

0.A.5   FIRMS MUST document their policies and procedures used in establishing and maintaining compliance with the GIPS standards, including ensuring the existence and ownership of client assets, and MUST apply them consistently.

0.A.6   If the FIRM does not meet all the REQUIREMENTS of the GIPS standards, the FIRM MUST NOT represent or state that it is "in compliance with the Global Investment Performance Standards except for . . ." or make any other statements that may indicate partial compliance with the GIPS standards.

0.A.7   Statements referring to the calculation methodology as being "in accordance," "in compliance," or "consistent" with the Global Investment Performance Standards, or similar statements, are prohibited.

0.A.8   Statements referring to the performance of a single, existing client PORTFOLIO as being "calculated in accordance with the Global Investment Performance Standards" are prohibited, except when a GIPS-compliant FIRM reports the performance of an individual client's PORTFOLIO to that client.

0.A.9   FIRMS MUST make every reasonable effort to provide a COMPLIANT PRESENTATION to all PROSPECTIVE CLIENTS. FIRMS MUST NOT choose to whom they present a COMPLIANT PRESENTATION. As long as a PROSPECTIVE CLIENT has received a COMPLIANT PRESENTATION within the previous 12 months, the FIRM has met this REQUIREMENT.

0.A.10   FIRMS MUST provide a complete list of COMPOSITE DESCRIPTIONS to any PROSPECTIVE CLIENT that makes such a request. FIRMS MUST include terminated COMPOSITES on the FIRM's list of COMPOSITE DESCRIPTIONS for at least five years after the COMPOSITE TERMINATION DATE.

0.A.11   FIRMS MUST provide a COMPLIANT PRESENTATION for any COMPOSITE listed on the FIRM's list of COMPOSITE DESCRIPTIONS to any PROSPECTIVE CLIENT that makes such a request.

0.A.12   FIRMS MUST be defined as an investment firm, subsidiary, or division held out to clients or PROSPECTIVE CLIENTS as a DISTINCT BUSINESS ENTITY.

0.A.13 For periods beginning on or after 1 January 2011, TOTAL FIRM ASSETS MUST be the aggregate FAIR VALUE of all discretionary and non-discretionary assets managed by the FIRM. This includes both fee-paying and non-fee-paying PORTFOLIOS.[1]

0.A.14 TOTAL FIRM ASSETS MUST include assets assigned to a SUB-ADVISOR provided the FIRM has discretion over the selection of the SUB-ADVISOR.

0.A.15 Changes in a FIRM's organization MUST NOT lead to alteration of historical COMPOSITE performance.

0.A.16 When the FIRM jointly markets with other firms, the FIRM claiming compliance with the GIPS standards MUST be sure that it is clearly defined and separate relative to other firms being marketed, and that it is clear which FIRM is claiming compliance.

Fundamentals of Compliance—Recommendations

0.B.1 FIRMS SHOULD comply with the RECOMMENDATIONS of the GIPS standards, including RECOMMENDATIONS in any updates, Guidance Statements, interpretations, Questions & Answers (Q&As), and clarifications published by CFA Institute and the GIPS Executive Committee, which will be made available on the GIPS website (www.gipsstandards.org) as well as in the *GIPS Handbook.*

0.B.2 FIRMS SHOULD be verified.

0.B.3 FIRMS SHOULD adopt the broadest, most meaningful definition of the FIRM. The scope of this definition SHOULD include all geographical (country, regional, etc.) offices operating under the same brand name regardless of the actual name of the individual investment management company.

0.B.4 FIRMS SHOULD provide to each existing client, on an annual basis, a COMPLIANT PRESENTATION of the COMPOSITE in which the client's PORTFOLIO is included.

1 Input Data

Input Data—Requirements

1.A.1 All data and information necessary to support all items included in a COMPLIANT PRESENTATION MUST be captured and maintained.

1.A.2 For periods beginning on or after 1 January 2011, PORTFOLIOS MUST be valued in accordance with the definition of FAIR VALUE and the GIPS Valuation Principles.[2]

1.A.3 FIRMS MUST value PORTFOLIOS in accordance with the COMPOSITE-specific valuation policy. PORTFOLIOS MUST be valued:

a For periods beginning on or after 1 January 2001, at least monthly.[3]

b For periods beginning on or after 1 January 2010, on the date of all LARGE CASH FLOWS. FIRMS MUST define LARGE CASH FLOW for each COMPOSITE to determine when PORTFOLIOS in that COMPOSITE MUST be valued.

c No more frequently than required by the valuation policy.

1.A.4 For periods beginning on or after 1 January 2010, FIRMS MUST value PORTFOLIOS as of the calendar month end or the last business day of the month.

1.A.5 For periods beginning on or after 1 January 2005, FIRMS MUST use TRADE DATE ACCOUNTING.

1.A.6 ACCRUAL ACCOUNTING MUST be used for fixed-income securities and all other investments that earn interest income. The value of fixed-income securities MUST include accrued income.

1.A.7 For periods beginning on or after 1 January 2006, COMPOSITES MUST have consistent beginning and ending annual valuation dates. Unless the COMPOSITE is reported on a non-calendar fiscal year, the beginning and ending valuation dates MUST be at calendar year end or on the last business day of the year.

---

1 For periods prior to 1 January 2011, TOTAL FIRM ASSETS MUST be the aggregate of the MARKET VALUE of all discretionary and non-discretionary assets under management within the defined FIRM.
2 For periods prior to 1 January 2011, portfolio valuations MUST be based on MARKET VALUES (not cost basis or book values).
3 For periods prior to 1 January 2001, PORTFOLIOS MUST be valued at least quarterly.

Input Data—Recommendations

1.B.1 FIRMS SHOULD value PORTFOLIOS on the date of all EXTERNAL CASH FLOWS.

1.B.2 Valuations SHOULD be obtained from a qualified independent third party.

1.B.3 ACCRUAL ACCOUNTING SHOULD be used for dividends (as of the ex-dividend date).

1.B.4 FIRMS SHOULD accrue INVESTMENT MANAGEMENT FEES.

2 Calculation Methodology

Calculation Methodology—Requirements

2.A.1 TOTAL RETURNS MUST be used.

2.A.2 FIRMS MUST calculate TIME-WEIGHTED RATES OF RETURN that adjust for EXTERNAL CASH FLOWS. Both periodic and sub-period returns MUST be geometrically LINKED. EXTERNAL CASH FLOWS MUST be treated according to the FIRM'S COMPOSITE-specific policy. At a minimum:

    a For periods beginning on or after 1 January 2001, FIRMS MUST calculate PORTFOLIO returns at least monthly.

    b For periods beginning on or after 1 January 2005, FIRMS MUST calculate PORTFOLIO returns that adjust for daily-weighted EXTERNAL CASH FLOWS.

2.A.3 Returns from cash and cash equivalents held in PORTFOLIOS MUST be included in all return calculations.

2.A.4 All returns MUST be calculated after the deduction of the actual TRADING EXPENSES incurred during the period. FIRMS MUST NOT use estimated TRADING EXPENSES.

2.A.5 If the actual TRADING EXPENSES cannot be identified and segregated from a BUNDLED FEE:

    a When calculating GROSS-OF-FEES returns, returns MUST be reduced by the entire BUNDLED FEE or the portion of the BUNDLED FEE that includes the TRADING EXPENSES. FIRMS MUST NOT use estimated TRADING EXPENSES.

    b When calculating NET-OF-FEES returns, returns MUST be reduced by the entire BUNDLED FEE or the portion of the BUNDLED FEE that includes the TRADING EXPENSES and the INVESTMENT MANAGEMENT FEE. FIRMS MUST NOT use estimated TRADING EXPENSES.

2.A.6 COMPOSITE returns MUST be calculated by asset-weighting the individual PORTFOLIO returns using beginning-of-period values or a method that reflects both beginning-of-period values and EXTERNAL CASH FLOWS.

2.A.7 COMPOSITE returns MUST be calculated:

    a For periods beginning on or after 1 January 2006, by asset-weighting the individual PORTFOLIO returns at least quarterly.

    b For periods beginning on or after 1 January 2010, by asset-weighting the individual PORTFOLIO returns at least monthly.

Calculation Methodology—Recommendations

2.B.1 Returns SHOULD be calculated net of non-reclaimable withholding taxes on dividends, interest, and capital gains. Reclaimable withholding taxes SHOULD be accrued.

2.B.2 For periods prior to 1 January 2010, FIRMS SHOULD calculate COMPOSITE returns by asset-weighting the individual PORTFOLIO returns at least monthly.

3 Composite Construction

Composite Construction—Requirements

3.A.1   All actual, fee-paying, discretionary PORTFOLIOS MUST be included in at least one COMPOSITE. Although non-fee-paying discretionary PORTFOLIOS may be included in a COMPOSITE (with appropriate disclosure), non-discretionary PORTFOLIOS MUST NOT be included in a FIRM'S COMPOSITES.

3.A.2   COMPOSITES MUST include only actual assets managed by the FIRM.

3.A.3   FIRMS MUST NOT LINK performance of simulated or model PORTFOLIOS with actual performance.

3.A.4   COMPOSITES MUST be defined according to investment mandate, objective, or strategy. COMPOSITES MUST include all PORTFOLIOS that meet the COMPOSITE DEFINITION. Any change to a COMPOSITE DEFINITION MUST NOT be applied retroactively. The COMPOSITE DEFINITION MUST be made available upon request.

3.A.5   COMPOSITES MUST include new PORTFOLIOS on a timely and consistent basis after each PORTFOLIO comes under management.

3.A.6   Terminated PORTFOLIOS MUST be included in the historical performance of the COMPOSITE up to the last full measurement period that each PORTFOLIO was under management.

3.A.7   PORTFOLIOS MUST NOT be switched from one COMPOSITE to another unless documented changes to a PORTFOLIO's investment mandate, objective, or strategy or the redefinition of the COMPOSITE makes it appropriate. The historical performance of the PORTFOLIO MUST remain with the original COMPOSITE.

3.A.8   For periods beginning on or after 1 January 2010, a CARVE-OUT MUST NOT be included in a COMPOSITE unless the CARVE-OUT is managed separately with its own cash balance.[4]

3.A.9   If the FIRM sets a minimum asset level for PORTFOLIOS to be included in a COMPOSITE, the FIRM MUST NOT include PORTFOLIOS below the minimum asset level in that COMPOSITE. Any changes to a COMPOSITE-specific minimum asset level MUST NOT be applied retroactively.

3.A.10   FIRMS that wish to remove PORTFOLIOS from COMPOSITES in cases of SIGNIFICANT CASH FLOWS MUST define "significant" on an EX-ANTE, COMPOSITE-specific basis and MUST consistently follow the COMPOSITE-specific policy.

Composite Construction—Recommendations

3.B.1   If the FIRM sets a minimum asset level for PORTFOLIOS to be included in a COMPOSITE, the FIRM SHOULD NOT present a COMPLIANT PRESENTATION of the composite to a PROSPECTIVE CLIENT known not to meet the COMPOSITE's minimum asset level.

3.B.2   To remove the effect of a SIGNIFICANT CASH FLOW, the FIRM SHOULD use a TEMPORARY NEW ACCOUNT.

4 Disclosure

Disclosure—Requirements

4.A.1   Once a FIRM has met all the REQUIREMENTS of the GIPS standards, the FIRM MUST disclose its compliance with the GIPS standards using one of the following compliance statements. The claim of compliance MUST only be used in a COMPLIANT PRESENTATION.

For FIRMS that are verified:

"[Insert name of FIRM] claims compliance with the Global Investment Performance Standards (GIPS®) and has prepared and presented this report in compliance with the GIPS standards. [Insert name of FIRM] has been independently verified for the periods [insert dates]. The verification report(s) is/are available upon request.

---

[4] For periods prior to 1 January 2010, if CARVE-OUTS were included in a COMPOSITE, cash MUST have been allocated to the CARVE-OUT in a timely and consistent manner.

Verification assesses whether (1) the firm has complied with all the composite construction requirements of the GIPS standards on a firm-wide basis and (2) the firm's policies and procedures are designed to calculate and present performance in compliance with the GIPS standards. Verification does not ensure the accuracy of any specific composite presentation."

For COMPOSITES of a verified FIRM that have also had a PERFORMANCE EXAMINATION:

"[Insert name of FIRM] claims compliance with the Global Investment Performance Standards (GIPS®) and has prepared and presented this report in compliance with the GIPS standards. [Insert name of FIRM] has been independently verified for the periods [insert dates].

Verification assesses whether (1) the firm has complied with all the composite construction requirements of the GIPS standards on a firm-wide basis and (2) the firm's policies and procedures are designed to calculate and present performance in compliance with the GIPS standards. The [insert name of COMPOSITE] composite has been examined for the periods [insert dates]. The verification and performance examination reports are available upon request."

For FIRMS that have not been verified:

"[Insert name of FIRM] claims compliance with the Global Investment Performance Standards (GIPS®) and has prepared and presented this report in compliance with the GIPS standards. [Insert name of FIRM] has not been independently verified."

4.A.2   FIRMS MUST disclose the definition of the FIRM used to determine TOTAL FIRM ASSETS and FIRM-wide compliance.

4.A.3   FIRMS MUST disclose the COMPOSITE DESCRIPTION.

4.A.4   FIRMS MUST disclose the BENCHMARK DESCRIPTION.

4.A.5   When presenting GROSS-OF-FEES returns, FIRMS MUST disclose if any other fees are deducted in addition to the TRADING EXPENSES.

4.A.6   When presenting NET-OF-FEES returns, FIRMS MUST disclose:

a   If any other fees are deducted in addition to the INVESTMENT MANAGEMENT FEES and TRADING EXPENSES;

b   If model or actual INVESTMENT MANAGEMENT FEES are used; and

c   If returns are net of any PERFORMANCE-BASED FEES.

4.A.7   FIRMS MUST disclose the currency used to express performance.

4.A.8   FIRMS MUST disclose which measure of INTERNAL DISPERSION is presented.

4.A.9   FIRMS MUST disclose the FEE SCHEDULE appropriate to the COMPLIANT PRESENTATION.

4.A.10 FIRMS MUST disclose the COMPOSITE CREATION DATE.

4.A.11 FIRMS MUST disclose that the FIRM's list of COMPOSITE DESCRIPTIONS is available upon request.

4.A.12 FIRMS MUST disclose that policies for valuing PORTFOLIOS, calculating performance, and preparing COMPLIANT PRESENTATIONS are available upon request.

4.A.13 FIRMS MUST disclose the presence, use, and extent of leverage, derivatives, and short positions, if material, including a description of the frequency of use and characteristics of the instruments sufficient to identify risks.

4.A.14 FIRMS MUST disclose all significant events that would help a PROSPECTIVE CLIENT interpret the COMPLIANT PRESENTATION.

4.A.15 For any performance presented for periods prior to 1 January 2000 that does not comply with the GIPS standards, FIRMS MUST disclose the periods of non-compliance.

4.A.16 If the FIRM is redefined, the FIRM MUST disclose the date of, description of, and reason for the redefinition.

4.A.17 If a COMPOSITE is redefined, the FIRM MUST disclose the date of, description of, and reason for the redefinition.

4.A.18 FIRMS MUST disclose changes to the name of a COMPOSITE.

4.A.19 FIRMS MUST disclose the minimum asset level, if any, below which PORTFOLIOS are not included in a COMPOSITE. FIRMS MUST also disclose any changes to the minimum asset level.

4.A.20 FIRMS MUST disclose relevant details of the treatment of withholding taxes on dividends, interest income, and capital gains, if material. FIRMS MUST also disclose if BENCHMARK returns are net of withholding taxes if this information is available.

4.A.21   For periods beginning on or after 1 January 2011, FIRMS MUST disclose and describe any known material differences in exchange rates or valuation sources used among the PORTFOLIOS within a COMPOSITE, and between the COMPOSITE and the BENCHMARK.[5]

4.A.22   If the COMPLIANT PRESENTATION conforms with laws and/or regulations that conflict with the REQUIREMENTS of the GIPS standards, FIRMS MUST disclose this fact and disclose the manner in which the laws and/or regulations conflict with the GIPS standards.

4.A.23   For periods prior to 1 January 2010, if CARVE-OUTS are included in a COMPOSITE, FIRMS MUST disclose the policy used to allocate cash to CARVE-OUTS.

4.A.24   If a COMPOSITE contains PORTFOLIOS with BUNDLED FEES, FIRMS MUST disclose the types of fees that are included in the BUNDLED FEE.

4.A.25   For periods beginning on or after 1 January 2006, FIRMS MUST disclose the use of a SUB-ADVISOR and the periods a SUB-ADVISOR was used.

4.A.26   For periods prior to 1 January 2010, FIRMS MUST disclose if any PORTFOLIOS were not valued at calendar month end or on the last business day of the month.

4.A.27   For periods beginning on or after 1 January 2011, FIRMS MUST disclose the use of subjective unobservable inputs for valuing PORTFOLIO investments (as described in the GIPS Valuation Principles) if the PORTFOLIO investments valued using subjective unobservable inputs are material to the COMPOSITE.

4.A.28   For periods beginning on or after 1 January 2011, FIRMS MUST disclose if the COMPOSITE's valuation hierarchy materially differs from the RECOMMENDED hierarchy in the GIPS Valuation Principles.

4.A.29   If the FIRM determines no appropriate BENCHMARK for the COMPOSITE exists, the FIRM MUST disclose why no BENCHMARK is presented.

4.A.30   If the FIRM changes the BENCHMARK, the FIRM MUST disclose the date of, description of, and reason for the change.

4.A.31   If a custom BENCHMARK or combination of multiple BENCHMARKS is used, the FIRM MUST disclose the BENCHMARK components, weights, and rebalancing process.

4.A.32   If the FIRM has adopted a SIGNIFICANT CASH FLOW policy for a specific COMPOSITE, the FIRM MUST disclose how the FIRM defines a SIGNIFICANT CASH FLOW for that COMPOSITE and for which periods.

4.A.33   FIRMS MUST disclose if the three-year annualized EX-POST STANDARD DEVIATION of the COMPOSITE and/or BENCHMARK is not presented because 36 monthly returns are not available.

4.A.34   If the FIRM determines that the three-year annualized EX-POST STANDARD DEVIATION is not relevant or appropriate, the FIRM MUST:

    a   Describe why EX-POST STANDARD DEVIATION is not relevant or appropriate; and

    b   Describe the additional risk measure presented and why it was selected.

4.A.35   FIRMS MUST disclose if the performance from a past firm or affiliation is LINKED to the performance of the FIRM.

Disclosure—Recommendations

4.B.1   FIRMS SHOULD disclose material changes to valuation policies and/or methodologies.

4.B.2   FIRMS SHOULD disclose material changes to calculation policies and/or methodologies.

4.B.3   FIRMS SHOULD disclose material differences between the BENCHMARK and the COMPOSITE's investment mandate, objective, or strategy.

4.B.4   FIRMS SHOULD disclose the key assumptions used to value PORTFOLIO investments.

4.B.5   If a parent company contains multiple firms, each FIRM within the parent company SHOULD disclose a list of the other firms contained within the parent company.

---

5 For periods prior to 1 January 2011, FIRMS MUST disclose and describe any known inconsistencies in the exchange rates used among the PORTFOLIOS within a COMPOSITE and between the COMPOSITE and the BENCHMARK.

4.B.6   For periods prior to 1 January 2011, FIRMS SHOULD disclose the use of subjective unobservable inputs for valuing PORTFOLIO investments (as described in the GIPS Valuation Principles) if the PORTFOLIO investments valued using subjective unobservable inputs are material to the COMPOSITE.

4.B.7   For periods prior to 1 January 2006, FIRMS SHOULD disclose the use of a SUB-ADVISOR and the periods a SUB-ADVISOR was used.

4.B.8   FIRMS SHOULD disclose if a COMPOSITE contains PROPRIETARY ASSETS.

5 Presentation and Reporting

Presentation and Reporting—Requirements

5.A.1   The following items MUST be presented in each COMPLIANT PRESENTATION:

a   At least five years of performance (or for the period since the FIRM'S inception or the COMPOSITE INCEPTION DATE if the FIRM or the COMPOSITE has been in existence less than five years) that meets the REQUIREMENTS of the GIPS standards. After a FIRM presents a minimum of five years of GIPS-compliant performance (or for the period since the FIRM'S inception or the COMPOSITE INCEPTION DATE if the FIRM or the COMPOSITE has been in existence less than five years), the FIRM MUST present an additional year of performance each year, building up to a minimum of 10 years of GIPS-compliant performance.

b   COMPOSITE returns for each annual period. COMPOSITE returns MUST be clearly identified as GROSS-OF-FEES or NET-OF-FEES.

c   For COMPOSITES with a COMPOSITE INCEPTION DATE of 1 January 2011 or later, when the initial period is less than a full year, returns from the COMPOSITE INCEPTION DATE through the initial annual period end.

d   For COMPOSITES with a COMPOSITE TERMINATION DATE of 1 January 2011 or later, returns from the last annual period end through the COMPOSITE TERMINATION DATE.

e   The TOTAL RETURN for the BENCHMARK for each annual period. The BENCHMARK MUST reflect the investment mandate, objective, or strategy of the COMPOSITE.

f   The number of PORTFOLIOS in the COMPOSITE as of each annual period end. If the COMPOSITE contains five or fewer PORTFOLIOS at period end, the number of PORTFOLIOS is not REQUIRED.

g   COMPOSITE assets as of each annual period end.

h   Either TOTAL FIRM ASSETS or COMPOSITE assets as a percentage of TOTAL FIRM ASSETS, as of each annual period end.

i   A measure of INTERNAL DISPERSION of individual PORTFOLIO returns for each annual period. If the COMPOSITE contains five or fewer PORTFOLIOS for the full year, a measure of INTERNAL DISPERSION is not REQUIRED.

5.A.2   For periods ending on or after 1 January 2011, FIRMS MUST present, as of each annual period end:

a   The three-year annualized EX-POST STANDARD DEVIATION (using monthly returns) of both the COMPOSITE and the BENCHMARK; and

b   An additional three-year EX-POST risk measure for the BENCHMARK (if available and appropriate) and the COMPOSITE, if the FIRM determines that the three-year annualized EX-POST STANDARD DEVIATION is not relevant or appropriate. The PERIODICITY of the COMPOSITE and the BENCHMARK MUST be identical when calculating the EX-POST risk measure.

5.A.3   FIRMS MUST NOT LINK non-GIPS-compliant performance for periods beginning on or after 1 January 2000 to their GIPS-compliant performance. FIRMS may LINK non-GIPS-compliant performance to GIPS-compliant performance provided that only GIPS-compliant performance is presented for periods beginning on or after 1 January 2000.

5.A.4   Returns for periods of less than one year MUST NOT be annualized.

5.A.5   For periods beginning on or after 1 January 2006 and ending prior to 1 January 2011, if a COMPOSITE includes CARVE-OUTS, the FIRM MUST present the percentage of COMPOSITE assets represented by CARVE-OUTS as of each annual period end.

5.A.6 If a COMPOSITE includes non-fee-paying PORTFOLIOS, the FIRM MUST present the percentage of COMPOSITE assets represented by non-fee-paying PORTFOLIOS as of each annual period end.

5.A.7 If a COMPOSITE includes PORTFOLIOS with BUNDLED FEES, the FIRM MUST present the percentage of COMPOSITE assets represented by PORTFOLIOS with BUNDLED FEES as of each annual period end.

5.A.8 **a** Performance of a past firm or affiliation MUST be LINKED to or used to represent the historical performance of a new or acquiring FIRM if, on a COMPOSITE-specific basis:

    i. Substantially all of the investment decision makers are employed by the new or acquiring FIRM (e.g., research department staff, portfolio managers, and other relevant staff);

    ii. The decision-making process remains substantially intact and independent within the new or acquiring FIRM; and

    iii. The new or acquiring FIRM has records that document and support the performance.

    b If a FIRM acquires another firm or affiliation, the FIRM has one year to bring any non-compliant assets into compliance.

Presentation and Reporting—Recommendations

5.B.1 FIRMS SHOULD present GROSS-OF-FEES returns.

5.B.2 FIRMS SHOULD present the following items:

    a Cumulative returns of the COMPOSITE and the BENCHMARK for all periods;

    b Equal-weighted mean and median COMPOSITE returns;

    c Quarterly and/or monthly returns; and

    d Annualized COMPOSITE and BENCHMARK returns for periods longer than 12 months.

5.B.3 For periods prior to 1 January 2011, FIRMS SHOULD present the three-year annualized EX-POST STANDARD DEVIATION (using monthly returns) of the COMPOSITE and the BENCHMARK as of each annual period end.

5.B.4 For each period for which an annualized EX-POST STANDARD DEVIATION of the COMPOSITE and the BENCHMARK are presented, the corresponding annualized return of the COMPOSITE and the BENCHMARK SHOULD also be presented.

5.B.5 For each period for which an annualized return of the COMPOSITE and the BENCHMARK are presented, the corresponding annualized EX-POST STANDARD DEVIATION (using monthly returns) of the COMPOSITE and the BENCHMARK SHOULD also be presented.

5.B.6 FIRMS SHOULD present additional relevant COMPOSITE-level EX-POST risk measures.

5.B.7 FIRMS SHOULD present more than 10 years of annual performance in the COMPLIANT PRESENTATION.

5.B.8 FIRMS SHOULD comply with the GIPS standards for all historical periods.

5.B.9 FIRMS SHOULD update COMPLIANT PRESENTATIONS quarterly.

6 Real Estate

Unless otherwise noted, the following REAL ESTATE provisions supplement the REQUIRED and RECOMMENDED provisions of the GIPS standards in Sections 0–5.

REAL ESTATE provisions were first included in the GIPS standards in 2005 and became effective 1 January 2006. All COMPLIANT PRESENTATIONS that included REAL ESTATE performance for periods beginning on or after 1 January 2006 were REQUIRED to meet all the REQUIREMENTS of the REAL ESTATE provisions of the 2005 edition of the GIPS standards. The following REAL ESTATE provisions are effective 1 January 2011. All REAL ESTATE COMPOSITES that include performance for periods beginning on or after 1 January 2011 MUST comply with all the REQUIREMENTS and SHOULD adhere to the RECOMMENDATIONS of the following REAL ESTATE provisions.

The following investment types are not considered REAL ESTATE and, therefore, MUST follow Sections 0–5 of the Global Investment Performance Standards:

- Publicly traded REAL ESTATE securities;

- Commercial mortgage-backed securities (CMBS); and

- Private debt investments, including commercial and residential loans where the expected return is solely related to contractual interest rates without any participation in the economic performance of the underlying REAL ESTATE.

Real Estate—Requirements

Input Data—Requirements (the following provisions do not apply: 1.A.3.a, 1.A.3.b, and 1.A.4)

6.A.1   For periods beginning on or after 1 January 2011, REAL ESTATE investments MUST be valued in accordance with the definition of FAIR VALUE and the GIPS Valuation Principles in Chapter II.[6]

6.A.2   For periods beginning on or after 1 January 2008, REAL ESTATE investments MUST be valued at least quarterly.[7]

6.A.3   For periods beginning on or after 1 January 2010, FIRMS MUST value PORTFOLIOS as of each quarter end or the last business day of each quarter.

6.A.4   REAL ESTATE investments MUST have an EXTERNAL VALUATION:

    a   For periods prior to 1 January 2012, at least once every 36 months.

    b   For periods beginning on or after 1 January 2012, at least once every 12 months unless client agreements stipulate otherwise, in which case REAL ESTATE investments MUST have an EXTERNAL VALUATION at least once every 36 months or per the client agreement if the client agreement requires EXTERNAL VALUATIONS more frequently than every 36 months.

6.A.5   EXTERNAL VALUATIONS must be performed by an independent external PROFESSIONALLY DESIGNATED, CERTIFIED, OR LICENSED COMMERCIAL PROPERTY VALUER/APPRAISER. In markets where these professionals are not available, the FIRM MUST take the necessary steps to ensure that only well-qualified independent property valuers or appraisers are used.

Calculation Methodology—Requirements (the following provisions do not apply: 2.A.2.a, 2.A.4, and 2.A.7)

6.A.6   FIRMS MUST calculate PORTFOLIO returns at least quarterly.

6.A.7   All returns MUST be calculated after the deduction of actual TRANSACTION EXPENSES incurred during the period.

6.A.8   For periods beginning on or after 1 January 2011, INCOME RETURNS and CAPITAL RETURNS (component returns) MUST be calculated separately using geometrically LINKED TIME-WEIGHTED RATES OF RETURN.

6.A.9   COMPOSITE TIME-WEIGHTED RATES OF RETURN, including component returns, MUST be calculated by asset-weighting the individual PORTFOLIO returns at least quarterly.

Disclosure—Requirements (the following provisions do not apply: 4.A.5, 4.A.6.a, 4.A.15, 4.A.26, 4.A.33, and 4.A.34)

6.A.10   The following items MUST be disclosed in each COMPLIANT PRESENTATION:

    a   The FIRM'S description of discretion;

    b   The INTERNAL VALUATION methodologies used to value REAL ESTATE investments for the most recent period;

    c   For periods beginning on or after 1 January 2011, material changes to valuation policies and/or methodologies;

    d   For periods beginning on or after 1 January 2011, material differences between an EXTERNAL VALUATION and the valuation used in performance reporting and the reason for the differences;

    e   The frequency REAL ESTATE investments are valued by an independent external PROFESSIONALLY DESIGNATED, CERTIFIED, OR LICENSED COMMERCIAL PROPERTY VALUER/APPRAISER;

---

[6] For periods prior to 1 January 2011, REAL ESTATE investments MUST be valued at MARKET VALUE (as previously defined for REAL ESTATE in the 2005 edition of the GIPS standards).

[7] For periods prior to 1 January 2008, REAL ESTATE investments MUST be valued at least once every 12 months.

f   When component returns are calculated separately using geometrically LINKED TIME-WEIGHTED RATES OF RETURN; and

g   For periods prior to 1 January 2011, if component returns are adjusted such that the sum of the INCOME RETURN and the CAPITAL RETURN equals the TOTAL RETURN.

6.A.11   For any performance presented for periods prior to 1 January 2006 that does not comply with the GIPS standards, FIRMS MUST disclose the periods of non-compliance.

6.A.12   When presenting GROSS-OF-FEES returns, FIRMS MUST disclose if any other fees are deducted in addition to the TRANSACTION EXPENSES.

6.A.13   When presenting NET-OF-FEES returns, FIRMS MUST disclose if any other fees are deducted in addition to the INVESTMENT MANAGEMENT FEES and TRANSACTION EXPENSES.

Presentation and Reporting—Requirements (the following provisions do not apply: 5.A.1.i, 5.A.2, and 5.A.3)

6.A.14   FIRMS MUST present component returns in addition to TOTAL RETURNS. COMPOSITE component returns MUST be clearly identified as GROSS-OF-FEES or NET-OF-FEES.

6.A.15   FIRMS MUST NOT LINK non-GIPS-compliant performance for periods beginning on or after 1 January 2006 to their GIPS-compliant performance. FIRMS may LINK non-GIPS-compliant performance to their GIPS-compliant performance provided that only GIPS-compliant performance is presented for periods beginning on or after 1 January 2006.

6.A.16   The following items MUST be presented in each COMPLIANT PRESENTATION:

a   As a measure of INTERNAL DISPERSION, high and low annual TIME-WEIGHTED RATES OF RETURN for the individual PORTFOLIOS in the COMPOSITE. If the COMPOSITE contains five or fewer PORTFOLIOS for the full year, a measure of INTERNAL DISPERSION is not REQUIRED.

b   As of each annual period end, the percentage of COMPOSITE assets valued using an EXTERNAL VALUATION during the annual period.

The following provisions are additional REQUIREMENTS for REAL ESTATE CLOSED-END FUND COMPOSITES:

Calculation Methodology—Requirements

6.A.17   FIRMS MUST calculate annualized SINCE INCEPTION INTERNAL RATES OF RETURN (SI-IRR).

6.A.18   The SI-IRR MUST be calculated using quarterly cash flows at a minimum.

Composite Construction—Requirements

6.A.19   COMPOSITES MUST be defined by VINTAGE YEAR and investment mandate, objective, or strategy. The COMPOSITE DEFINITION MUST remain consistent throughout the life of the COMPOSITE.

Disclosure—Requirements

6.A.20   FIRMS MUST disclose the FINAL LIQUIDATION DATE for liquidated COMPOSITES.

6.A.21   FIRMS MUST disclose the frequency of cash flows used in the SI-IRR calculation.

6.A.22   FIRMS MUST disclose the VINTAGE YEAR of the COMPOSITE and how the VINTAGE YEAR is defined.

Presentation and Reporting—Requirements

6.A.23   The following items MUST be presented in each COMPLIANT PRESENTATION:

a   FIRMS MUST present the NET-OF-FEES SI-IRR of the COMPOSITE through each annual period end. FIRMS MUST initially present at least five years of performance (or for the period since the FIRM'S inception or the COMPOSITE INCEPTION DATE if the FIRM or the COMPOSITE has been in existence less than five years) that meets the REQUIREMENTS of the GIPS standards. Each subsequent year, FIRMS MUST present an additional year of performance.

b   For periods beginning on or after 1 January 2011, when the initial period is less than a full year, FIRMS MUST present the non-annualized NET-OF-FEES SI-IRR through the initial annual period end.

c For periods ending on or after 1 January 2011, FIRMS MUST present the NET-OF-FEES SI-IRR through the COMPOSITE FINAL LIQUIDATION DATE.

6.A.24 If the GROSS-OF-FEES SI-IRR of the COMPOSITE is presented in the COMPLIANT PRESENTATION, FIRMS MUST present the GROSS-OF-FEES SI-IRR of the COMPOSITE for the same periods as the NET-OF-FEES SI-IRR is presented.

6.A.25 FIRMS MUST present, as of each annual period end:

a COMPOSITE SINCE INCEPTION PAID-IN CAPITAL;

b COMPOSITE SINCE INCEPTION DISTRIBUTIONS;

c COMPOSITE cumulative COMMITTED CAPITAL;

d TOTAL VALUE TO SINCE INCEPTION PAID-IN CAPITAL (INVESTMENT MULTIPLE or TVPI);

e SINCE INCEPTION DISTRIBUTIONS TO SINCE INCEPTION PAID-IN CAPITAL (REALIZATION MULTIPLE or DPI);

f SINCE INCEPTION PAID-IN CAPITAL TO cumulative COMMITTED CAPITAL (PIC MULTIPLE); and

g RESIDUAL VALUE TO SINCE INCEPTION PAID-IN CAPITAL (UNREALIZED MULTIPLE or RVPI).

6.A.26 FIRMS MUST present the SI-IRR of the BENCHMARK through each annual period end. The BENCHMARK MUST:

a Reflect the investment mandate, objective, or strategy of the COMPOSITE;

b Be presented for the same time period as presented for the COMPOSITE; and

c Be the same VINTAGE YEAR as the COMPOSITE.

Real Estate—Recommendations

Input Data—Recommendations (the following provision does not apply: 1.B.1)

6.B.1 For periods prior to 1 January 2012, REAL ESTATE investments SHOULD be valued by an independent external PROFESSIONALLY DESIGNATED, CERTIFIED, OR LICENSED COMMERCIAL PROPERTY VALUER/APPRAISER at least once every 12 months.

6.B.2 REAL ESTATE investments SHOULD be valued as of the annual period end by an independent external PROFESSIONALLY DESIGNATED, CERTIFIED, OR LICENSED COMMERCIAL PROPERTY VALUER/APPRAISER.

Disclosure—Recommendations

6.B.3 FIRMS SHOULD disclose the basis of accounting for the PORTFOLIOS in the COMPOSITE (e.g., US GAAP, IFRS).

6.B.4 FIRMS SHOULD explain and disclose material differences between the valuation used in performance reporting and the valuation used in financial reporting as of each annual period end.

6.B.5 For periods prior to 1 January 2011, FIRMS SHOULD disclose material changes to valuation policies and/or methodologies.

Presentation and Reporting—Recommendations (the following provisions do not apply: 5.B.3, 5.B.4, and 5.B.5)

6.B.6 FIRMS SHOULD present both GROSS-OF-FEES and NET-OF-FEES returns.

6.B.7 FIRMS SHOULD present the percentage of the total value of COMPOSITE assets that are not REAL ESTATE as of each annual period end.

6.B.8 FIRMS SHOULD present the component returns of the BENCHMARK, if available.

The following provision is an additional RECOMMENDATION **for** REAL ESTATE CLOSED-END FUND COMPOSITES**:**

Calculation Methodology—Recommendations

6.B.9 The SI-IRR SHOULD be calculated using daily cash flows.

7 Private Equity

Unless otherwise noted, the following PRIVATE EQUITY provisions supplement the REQUIRED and RECOMMENDED provisions of the GIPS standards in Sections 0–5.

PRIVATE EQUITY provisions were first included in the GIPS standards in 2005 and became effective 1 January 2006. All COMPLIANT PRESENTATIONS that included PRIVATE EQUITY performance for periods ending on or after 1 January 2006 were REQUIRED to meet all the REQUIREMENTS of the PRIVATE EQUITY provisions of the 2005 edition of the GIPS standards. The following PRIVATE EQUITY provisions are effective 1 January 2011. All PRIVATE EQUITY COMPOSITES that include performance for periods ending on or after 1 January 2011 MUST comply with all the REQUIREMENTS and SHOULD comply with the RECOMMENDATIONS of the following PRIVATE EQUITY provisions.

The following are provisions that apply to the calculation and presentation of PRIVATE EQUITY investments made by fixed life, fixed commitment PRIVATE EQUITY investment vehicles including PRIMARY FUNDS and FUNDS OF FUNDS. These provisions also apply to fixed life, fixed commitment SECONDARY FUNDS, which MUST apply either the provisions applicable to PRIMARY FUNDS or the provisions applicable to FUNDS OF FUNDS, depending on which form the SECONDARY FUND uses to make investments. PRIVATE EQUITY OPEN-END and EVERGREEN FUNDS MUST follow Sections 0–5 in the Provisions of the Global Investment Performance Standards. REAL ESTATE CLOSED-END FUNDS MUST follow Section 6 in the Provisions of the Global Investment Performance Standards.

Private Equity—Requirements

Input Data—Requirements (the following provisions do not apply: 1.A.3.a, 1.A.3.b, and 1.A.4)

7.A.1   For periods ending on or after 1 January 2011, PRIVATE EQUITY investments MUST be valued in accordance with the definition of FAIR VALUE and the GIPS Valuation Principles in Chapter II.[8]

7.A.2   PRIVATE EQUITY investments MUST be valued at least annually.

Calculation Methodology—Requirements (the following provisions do not apply: 2.A.2, 2.A.4, 2.A.6, and 2.A.7)

7.A.3   FIRMS MUST calculate annualized SINCE INCEPTION INTERNAL RATES OF RETURN (SI-IRR).

7.A.4   For periods ending on or after 1 January 2011, the SI-IRR MUST be calculated using daily cash flows. Stock DISTRIBUTIONS MUST be included as cash flows and MUST be valued at the time of DISTRIBUTION.[9]

7.A.5   All returns MUST be calculated after the deduction of actual TRANSACTION EXPENSES incurred during the period.

7.A.6   NET-OF-FEES returns MUST be net of actual INVESTMENT MANAGEMENT FEES (including CARRIED INTEREST).

7.A.7   For FUNDS OF FUNDS, all returns MUST be net of all underlying partnership and/or fund fees and expenses, including CARRIED INTEREST.

Composite Construction—Requirements (the following provision does not apply: 3.A.10)

7.A.8   COMPOSITE DEFINITIONS MUST remain consistent throughout the life of the COMPOSITE.

7.A.9   PRIMARY FUNDS MUST be included in at least one COMPOSITE defined by VINTAGE YEAR and investment mandate, objective, or strategy.

7.A.10   FUNDS OF FUNDS MUST be included in at least one COMPOSITE defined by VINTAGE YEAR of the FUND OF FUNDS and/or investment mandate, objective, or strategy.

Disclosure—Requirements (the following provisions do not apply: 4.A.5, 4.A.6.a, 4.A.6.b, 4.A.8, 4.A.15, 4.A.26, 4.A.32, 4.A.33, and 4.A.34)

7.A.11   FIRMS MUST disclose the VINTAGE YEAR of the COMPOSITE and how the VINTAGE YEAR is defined.

7.A.12   FIRMS MUST disclose the FINAL LIQUIDATION DATE for liquidated COMPOSITES.

---

8 For periods ending prior to 1 January 2011, PRIVATE EQUITY investments MUST be valued according to either the GIPS Private Equity Valuation Principles in Appendix D of the 2005 edition of the GIPS standards or the GIPS Valuation Principles in the 2010 edition of the GIPS standards.

9 For periods ending prior to 1 January 2011, the SI-IRR MUST be calculated using either daily or monthly cash flows.

7.A.13   FIRMS MUST disclose the valuation methodologies used to value PRIVATE EQUITY investments for the most recent period.

7.A.14   For periods ending on or after 1 January 2011, FIRMS MUST disclose material changes to valuation policies and/or methodologies.

7.A.15   If the FIRM adheres to any industry valuation guidelines in addition to the GIPS Valuation Principles, the FIRM MUST disclose which guidelines have been applied.

7.A.16   FIRMS MUST disclose the calculation methodology used for the BENCHMARK. If FIRMS present the PUBLIC MARKET EQUIVALENT of a COMPOSITE as a BENCHMARK, FIRMS MUST disclose the index used to calculate the PUBLIC MARKET EQUIVALENT.

7.A.17   FIRMS MUST disclose the frequency of cash flows used in the SI-IRR calculation if daily cash flows are not used for periods prior to 1 January 2011.

7.A.18   For GROSS-OF-FEES returns, FIRMS MUST disclose if any other fees are deducted in addition to the TRANS-ACTION EXPENSES.

7.A.19   For NET-OF-FEES returns, FIRMS MUST disclose if any other fees are deducted in addition to the INVESTMENT MANAGEMENT FEES and transaction expenses.

7.A.20   For any performance presented for periods ending prior to 1 January 2006 that does not comply with the GIPS standards, FIRMS MUST disclose the periods of non-compliance.

Presentation and Reporting—Requirements (the following provisions do not apply: 5.A.1.a, 5.A.1.b, 5.A.1.c, 5.A.1.d, 5.A.1.e, 5.A.1.i, 5.A.2, and 5.A.3)

7.A.21   The following items MUST be presented in each COMPLIANT PRESENTATION:

    a   FIRMS MUST present both the NET-OF-FEES and GROSS-OF-FEES SI-IRR of the COMPOSITE through each annual period end. FIRMS MUST initially present at least five years of performance (or for the period since the FIRM's inception or the COMPOSITE INCEPTION DATE if the FIRM or the COMPOSITE has been in existence less than five years) that meets the REQUIREMENTS of the GIPS standards. Each subsequent year, FIRMS MUST present an additional year of performance. Composite returns MUST be clearly identified as GROSS-OF-FEES or NET-OF-FEES.

    b   For periods beginning on or after 1 January 2011, when the initial period is less than a full year, FIRMS MUST present the non-annualized NET-OF-FEES and GROSS-OF-FEES SI-IRR through the initial annual period end.

    c   For periods ending on or after 1 January 2011, FIRMS MUST present the NET-OF-FEES and GROSS-OF-FEES SI-IRR through the COMPOSITE FINAL LIQUIDATION DATE.

7.A.22   For periods ending on or after 1 January 2011, for FUND OF FUNDS COMPOSITES, if the COMPOSITE is defined only by investment mandate, objective, or strategy, FIRMS MUST also present the SI-IRR of the underlying investments aggregated by VINTAGE YEAR as well as other measures as REQUIRED in 7.A.23. These measures MUST be presented gross of the FUND OF FUNDS INVESTMENT MANAGEMENT FEES and MUST be presented as of the most recent annual period end.

7.A.23   FIRMS MUST present as of each annual period end:

    a   Composite since inception paid-in capital;

    b   Composite since inception distributions;

    c   Composite cumulative committed capital;

    d   Total value to since inception paid-in capital (investment multiple or TVPI);

    e   Since inception distributions to since inception paid-in capital (realization multiple or DPI);

    f   Since inception paid-in capital to cumulative committed capital (PIC multiple); and

    g   Residual value to since inception paid-in capital (unrealized multiple or RVPI).

7.A.24   FIRMS MUST present the SI-IRR for the BENCHMARK through each annual period end. The BENCHMARK MUST:

    a   Reflect the investment mandate, objective, or strategy of the COMPOSITE;

    b   Be presented for the same time periods as presented for the COMPOSITE; and

    c   Be the same VINTAGE YEAR as the COMPOSITE.

7.A.25   For FUND OF FUNDS COMPOSITES, if the COMPOSITE is defined only by investment mandate, objective, or strategy and a BENCHMARK is presented for the underlying investments, the BENCHMARK MUST be the same VINTAGE YEAR and investment mandate, objective, or strategy as the underlying investments.

7.A.26   For periods ending on or after 1 January 2011, for FUND OF FUNDS COMPOSITES, FIRMS MUST present the percentage, if any, of COMPOSITE assets that is invested in DIRECT INVESTMENTS (rather than in fund investment vehicles) as of each annual period end.

7.A.27   For periods ending on or after 1 January 2011, for PRIMARY FUND COMPOSITES, FIRMS MUST present the percentage, if any, of COMPOSITE assets that is invested in fund investment vehicles (rather than in DIRECT INVESTMENTS) as of each annual period end.

7.A.28   FIRMS MUST NOT present non-GIPS-compliant performance for periods ending on or after 1 January 2006. For periods ending prior to 1 January 2006, FIRMS may present non-GIPS-compliant performance.

Private Equity—Recommendations

Input Data—Recommendations (the following provision does not apply: 1.B.1)

7.B.1   PRIVATE EQUITY investments SHOULD be valued at least quarterly.

Calculation Methodology—Recommendations (the following provision does not apply: 2.B.2)

7.B.2   For periods ending prior to 1 January 2011, the SI-IRR SHOULD be calculated using daily cash flows.

Composite Construction—Recommendations (the following provision does not apply: 3.B.2)

Disclosure—Recommendations

7.B.3   FIRMS SHOULD explain and disclose material differences between the valuations used in performance reporting and the valuations used in financial reporting as of each annual period end.

7.B.4   For periods prior to 1 January 2011, FIRMS SHOULD disclose material changes to valuation policies and/or methodologies.

Presentation and Reporting—Recommendations (the following provisions do not apply: 5.B.2, 5.B.3, 5.B.4, and 5.B.5)

7.B.5   For periods ending on or after 1 January 2011, for FUND OF FUNDS COMPOSITES, if the COMPOSITE is defined only by VINTAGE YEAR of the FUND OF FUNDS, FIRMS SHOULD also present the SI-IRR of the underlying investments aggregated by investment mandate, objective, or strategy and other measures as listed in 7.A.23. These measures SHOULD be presented gross of the FUND OF FUNDS INVESTMENT MANAGEMENT FEES.

7.B.6   For periods ending prior to 1 January 2011, for FUND OF FUNDS COMPOSITES, FIRMS SHOULD present the percentage, if any, of COMPOSITE assets that is invested in DIRECT INVESTMENTS (rather than in fund investment vehicles) as of each annual period end.

7.B.7   For periods ending prior to 1 January 2011, for PRIMARY FUND COMPOSITES, FIRMS SHOULD present the percentage, if any, of COMPOSITE assets that is invested in fund investment vehicles (rather than in DIRECT INVESTMENTS) as of each annual period end.

8 Wrap Fee/Separately Managed Account (SMA) Portfolios

The following provisions apply to the calculation and presentation of performance when presenting a COMPLIANT PRESENTATION to a WRAP FEE/SMA PROSPECTIVE CLIENT (which includes prospective WRAP FEE/SMA sponsors, prospective WRAP FEE/SMA clients, and existing WRAP FEE/SMA sponsors). Unless otherwise noted, the following WRAP FEE/SMA provisions supplement all the REQUIRED and RECOMMENDED provisions of the GIPS standards in Sections 0 5.

Although there are different types of WRAP FEE/SMA structures, these provisions apply to all WRAP FEE/SMA PORTFOLIOS where there are BUNDLED FEES and the WRAP FEE/SMA sponsor serves as an intermediary between the FIRM and the end user of the investment services. These provisions are not applicable to PORTFOLIOS defined as other types of BUNDLED FEE PORTFOLIOS. These provisions are also not applicable to model PORTFOLIOS that are provided by a FIRM to a WRAP FEE/SMA sponsor if the FIRM does not have discretionary PORTFOLIO management responsibility for the individual WRAP FEE/SMA PORTFOLIOS. Similarly, a FIRM or overlay manager in a Multiple Strategy Portfolio (MSP) or similar program is also excluded from applying these provisions to such PORTFOLIOS if they do not have discretion.

All WRAP FEE/SMA COMPLIANT PRESENTATIONS that include performance results for periods beginning on or after 1 January 2006 MUST meet all the REQUIREMENTS of the following WRAP FEE/SMA provisions.

Wrap Fee/SMA Requirements

Composite Construction—Requirements

8.A.1 FIRMS MUST include the performance record of actual WRAP FEE/SMA PORTFOLIOS in appropriate COMPOSITES in accordance with the FIRM's established PORTFOLIO inclusion policies. Once established, these COMPOSITES (containing actual WRAP FEE/SMA PORTFOLIOS) MUST be used in the FIRM's COMPLIANT PRESENTATIONS presented to WRAP FEE/SMA PROSPECTIVE CLIENTS.

Disclosure—Requirements (the following provision does not apply: 4.A.15)

8.A.2 For all WRAP FEE/SMA COMPLIANT PRESENTATIONS that include periods prior to the inclusion of an actual WRAP FEE/SMA PORTFOLIO in the COMPOSITE, the FIRM MUST disclose, for each period presented, that the COMPOSITE does not contain actual WRAP FEE/SMA PORTFOLIOS.

8.A.3 For any performance presented for periods prior to 1 January 2006 that does not comply with the GIPS standards, FIRMS MUST disclose the periods of non-compliance.

8.A.4 When FIRMS present COMPOSITE performance to an existing WRAP FEE/SMA sponsor that includes only that sponsor's WRAP FEE/SMA PORTFOLIOS (resulting in a "sponsor-specific COMPOSITE"):

   a FIRMS MUST disclose the name of the WRAP FEE/SMA sponsor represented by the sponsor-specific COMPOSITE; and

   b If the sponsor-specific COMPOSITE COMPLIANT PRESENTATION is intended for the purpose of generating WRAP FEE/SMA business and does not include performance net of the entire WRAP FEE, the COMPLIANT PRESENTATION MUST disclose that the named sponsor-specific COMPLIANT PRESENTATION is only for the use of the named WRAP FEE/SMA sponsor.

Presentation and Reporting—Requirements (the following provision does not apply: 5.A.3)

8.A.5 When FIRMS present performance to a WRAP FEE/SMA PROSPECTIVE CLIENT, the COMPOSITE presented MUST include the performance of all actual WRAP FEE/SMA PORTFOLIOS, if any, managed according to the COMPOSITE investment mandate, objective, or strategy, regardless of the WRAP FEE/SMA sponsor (resulting in a "style-defined COMPOSITE").

8.A.6 When FIRMS present performance to a WRAP FEE/SMA PROSPECTIVE CLIENT, performance MUST be presented net of the entire WRAP FEE.

8.A.7 FIRMS MUST NOT LINK non-GIPS-compliant performance for periods beginning on or after 1 January 2006 to their GIPS-compliant performance. FIRMS may LINK non-GIPS-compliant performance to their GIPS-compliant performance provided that only GIPS-compliant performance is presented for periods beginning on or after 1 January 2006.

II. GIPS VALUATION PRINCIPLES

The GIPS standards are based on the ethical principles of fair representation and full disclosure. In order for the performance calculations to be meaningful, the valuations of PORTFOLIO investments must have integrity and fairly reflect their value. Effective 1 January 2011, the GIPS standards REQUIRE FIRMS to apply a FAIR VALUE methodology following the definition and REQUIREMENTS listed below. The GIPS Valuation Principles, including the definition of FAIR VALUE, were developed with consideration of the work done by the International Accounting Standards Board (IASB) and the Financial Accounting Standards Board (FASB) as well as other organizations.

The shift to a broader FAIR VALUE REQUIREMENT has implications for all FIRMS claiming compliance with the GIPS standards. For liquid securities in active markets, the change to FAIR VALUE from MARKET VALUE will typically not result in a change to valuations. FIRMS MUST use the objective, observable, unadjusted quoted market prices for identical investments on the measurement date, if available.

Markets are not always liquid and investment prices are not always objective and/or observable. For illiquid or hard to value investments, or for investments where no observable MARKET VALUE or market price is available, additional steps are necessary. A FIRM's valuation policies and procedures MUST address situations where the market prices may be available for similar but not identical investments, inputs to valuations are subjective rather than objective, and/or markets are inactive instead of active. There is a RECOMMENDED valuation hierarchy in Section C below. FIRMS MUST disclose if the COMPOSITE's valuation hierarchy materially differs from the RECOMMENDED valuation hierarchy.

Although a FIRM may use external third parties to value investments, the FIRM still retains responsibility for compliance with the GIPS standards, including the GIPS Valuation Principles.

FIRMS claiming compliance with the GIPS standards MUST adhere to all the REQUIREMENTS and SHOULD comply with the RECOMMENDATIONS below.

Fair Value Definition

FAIR VALUE is defined as the amount at which an investment could be exchanged in a current arm's length transaction between willing parties in which the parties each act knowledgeably and prudently. The valuation MUST be determined using the objective, observable, unadjusted quoted market price for an identical investment in an active market on the measurement date, if available. In the absence of an objective, observable, unadjusted quoted market price for an identical investment in an active market on the measurement date, the valuation MUST represent the FIRM's best estimate of the MARKET VALUE. FAIR VALUE MUST include accrued income.

Valuation Requirements

FIRMS MUST comply with the following valuation REQUIREMENTS:

1   For periods beginning on or after 1 January 2011, PORTFOLIOS MUST be valued in accordance with the definition of FAIR VALUE and the GIPS Valuation Principles (Provision 1.A.2) Chapter II.

2   FIRMS MUST value investments using objective, observable, unadjusted quoted market prices for identical investments in active markets on the measurement date, if available.

3   FIRMS MUST comply with all applicable laws and regulations regarding the calculation and presentation of performance (Provision 0.A.2). Accordingly, FIRMS MUST comply with applicable laws and regulations relating to valuation.

4   If the COMPLIANT PRESENTATION conforms with laws and/or regulations that conflict with the REQUIREMENTS of the GIPS standards, FIRMS MUST disclose this fact and disclose the manner in which the laws and/or regulations conflict with the GIPS standards (Provision 4.A.22). This includes any conflicts between laws and/or regulations and the GIPS Valuation Principles.

5   FIRMS MUST document their policies and procedures used in establishing and maintaining compliance with the GIPS standards, including ensuring the existence and ownership of client assets, and MUST apply them consistently (Provision 0.A.5). Accordingly, FIRMS MUST document their valuation policies, procedures, methodologies, and hierarchy, including any changes, and MUST apply them consistently.

6   FIRMS MUST disclose that policies for valuing PORTFOLIOS, calculating performance, and preparing COMPLIANT PRESENTATIONS are available upon request (Provision 4.A.12).

7   For periods beginning on or after 1 January 2011, FIRMS MUST disclose the use of subjective unobservable inputs for valuing PORTFOLIO investments (as described in the GIPS Valuation Principles) if the PORTFOLIO investments valued using subjective unobservable inputs are material to the COMPOSITE (Provision 4.A.27).

8   For periods beginning on or after 1 January 2011, FIRMS MUST disclose if the COMPOSITE's valuation hierarchy materially differs from the RECOMMENDED hierarchy in the GIPS Valuation Principles (Provision 4.A.28).

Additional Real Estate Valuation Requirements

9   REAL ESTATE investments MUST have an EXTERNAL VALUATION (Provision 6.A.4).

10   The EXTERNAL VALUATION process MUST adhere to practices of the relevant valuation governing and standard setting body.

11   The FIRM MUST NOT use EXTERNAL VALUATIONS where the valuer's or appraiser's fee is contingent upon the investment's appraised value.

12   EXTERNAL VALUATIONS must be performed by an independent external PROFESSIONALLY DESIGNATED, CERTIFIED, OR LICENSED COMMERCIAL PROPERTY VALUER/APPRAISER. In markets where these professionals are not available, the FIRM MUST take necessary steps to ensure that only well-qualified independent property valuers or appraisers are used (Provision 6.A.5).

13   Firms MUST disclose the INTERNAL VALUATION methodologies used to value REAL ESTATE investments for the most recent period (Provision 6.A.10.b).

14   For periods beginning on or after 1 January 2011, FIRMS MUST disclose material changes to valuation policies and/or methodologies (Provision 6.A.10.c).

15   For periods beginning on or after 1 January 2011, FIRMS MUST disclose material differences between an EXTERNAL VALUATION and the valuation used in performance reporting and the reason for the differences (Provision 6.A.10.d).

16   Firms MUST present, as of each annual period end, the percentage of COMPOSITE assets valued using an EXTERNAL VALUATION during the annual period (Provision 6.A.16.b).

Additional Private Equity Valuation Requirements

17   The valuation methodology selected MUST be the most appropriate for a particular investment based on the nature, facts, and circumstances of the investment.

18   Firms MUST disclose the valuation methodologies used to value PRIVATE EQUITY investments for the most recent period (Provision 7.A.13).

19   For periods ending on or after 1 January 2011, FIRMS MUST disclose material changes to valuation policies and/or methodologies (Provision 7.A.14).

20   If the FIRM adheres to any industry valuation guidelines in addition to the GIPS Valuation Principles, the FIRM MUST disclose which guidelines have been applied (Provision 7.A.15).

Valuation Recommendations

FIRMS SHOULD comply with the following valuation RECOMMENDATIONS:

1   **Valuation Hierarchy**: FIRMS SHOULD incorporate the following hierarchy into the policies and procedures for determining FAIR VALUE for PORTFOLIO investments on a COMPOSITE-specific basis.

   a   Investments MUST be valued using objective, observable, unadjusted quoted market prices for identical investments in active markets on the measurement date, if available. If not available, then investments SHOULD be valued using;

   b   Objective, observable quoted market prices for similar investments in active markets. If not available or appropriate, then investments SHOULD be valued using;

c   Quoted prices for identical or similar investments in markets that are not active (markets in which there are few transactions for the investment, the prices are not current, or price quotations vary substantially over time and/or between market makers). If not available or appropriate, then investments SHOULD be valued based on;

d   Market-based inputs, other than quoted prices, that are observable for the investment. If not available or appropriate, then investments SHOULD be valued based on;

e   Subjective unobservable inputs for the investment where markets are not active at the measurement date. Unobservable inputs SHOULD only be used to measure FAIR VALUE to the extent that observable inputs and prices are not available or appropriate. Unobservable inputs reflect the FIRM's own assumptions about the assumptions that market participants would use in pricing the investment and SHOULD be developed based on the best information available under the circumstances.

2   FIRMS SHOULD disclose material changes to valuation policies and/or methodologies (Provision 4.B.1).

3   FIRMS SHOULD disclose the key assumptions used to value PORTFOLIO investments (Provision 4.B.4).

4   For periods prior to 1 January 2011, FIRMS SHOULD disclose the use of subjective unobservable inputs for valuing PORTFOLIO investments (as described in the GIPS Valuation Principles in Chapter II) if the PORTFOLIO investments valued using subjective unobservable inputs are material to the COMPOSITE (Provision 4.B.6).

5   Valuations SHOULD be obtained from a qualified independent third party (Provision 1.B.2).

Additional Real Estate Valuation Recommendations

6   Although appraisal standards may allow for a range of estimated values, it is RECOMMENDED that a single value be obtained from external valuers or appraisers because only one value is used in performance reporting.

7   It is RECOMMENDED that the external appraisal firm be rotated every three to five years.

8   FIRMS SHOULD explain and disclose material differences between the valuation used in performance reporting and the valuation used in financial reporting as of each annual period end (Provision 6.B.4).

9   For periods prior to 1 January 2011, FIRMS SHOULD disclose material changes to valuation policies and/or methodologies (Provision 6.B.5).

Additional Private Equity Valuation Recommendations

10   FIRMS SHOULD explain and disclose material differences between the valuations used in performance reporting and the valuations used in financial reporting as of each annual period end (Provision 7.B.3).

11   For periods prior to 1 January 2011, FIRMS SHOULD disclose material changes to valuation policies and/or methodologies (Provision 7.B.4).

12   The following considerations SHOULD be incorporated into the valuation process:

a   The quality and reliability of the data used in each methodology;

b   The comparability of enterprise or transaction data;

c   The stage of development of the enterprise; and

d   Any additional considerations unique to the enterprise.

III. GIPS ADVERTISING GUIDELINES

Purpose of the GIPS Advertising Guidelines

The GIPS Advertising Guidelines provide FIRMS with options for advertising performance when mentioning the FIRM's claim of compliance. The GIPS Advertising Guidelines do not replace the GIPS standards, nor do they absolve FIRMS from presenting a COMPLIANT PRESENTATION as REQUIRED by the GIPS standards. These guidelines only apply to FIRMS that already satisfy all the REQUIREMENTS of the GIPS standards on a FIRM-wide basis and claim compliance with the GIPS standards in an advertisement. FIRMS that choose to claim compliance in an advertisement MUST follow the GIPS Advertising Guidelines or include a COMPLIANT PRESENTATION in the advertisement.

Definition of Advertisement

For the purposes of these guidelines, an advertisement includes any materials that are distributed to or designed for use in newspapers, magazines, FIRM brochures, letters, media, websites, or any other written or electronic material addressed to more than one PROSPECTIVE CLIENT. Any written material, other than one-on-one presentations and individual client reporting, distributed to maintain existing clients or solicit new clients for a FIRM is considered an advertisement.

Relationship of GIPS Advertising Guidelines to Regulatory Requirements

FIRMS advertising performance MUST adhere to all applicable laws and regulations governing advertisements. FIRMS are encouraged to seek legal or regulatory counsel because additional disclosures may be REQUIRED. In cases where applicable laws and/or regulations conflict with the REQUIREMENTS of the GIPS standards and/or the GIPS Advertising Guidelines, FIRMS are REQUIRED to comply with the law or regulation.

The calculation and advertisement of pooled unitized investment vehicles, such as mutual funds and open-ended investment companies, are regulated in most markets. The GIPS Advertising Guidelines are not intended to replace applicable laws and/or regulations when a FIRM is advertising performance solely for a pooled unitized investment vehicle.

Other Information

The advertisement may include other information beyond what is REQUIRED under the GIPS Advertising Guidelines provided the information is shown with equal or lesser prominence relative to the information REQUIRED by the GIPS Advertising Guidelines and the information does not conflict with the REQUIREMENTS of the GIPS standards and/or the GIPS Advertising Guidelines. FIRMS MUST adhere to the principles of fair representation and full disclosure when advertising and MUST NOT present performance or performance-related information that is false or misleading.

Requirements of the GIPS Advertising Guidelines

All advertisements that include a claim of compliance with the GIPS standards by following the GIPS Advertising Guidelines MUST disclose the following:

1   The definition of the FIRM.

2   How a PROSPECTIVE CLIENT can obtain a COMPLIANT PRESENTATION and/or the FIRM's list of COMPOSITE DESCRIPTIONS.

3   The GIPS compliance statement for advertisements:

> "[Insert name of FIRM] claims compliance with the Global Investment Performance Standards (GIPS®)."

All advertisements that include a claim of compliance with the GIPS standards by following the GIPS Advertising Guidelines and that present performance MUST also disclose the following information, which MUST be taken or derived from a COMPLIANT PRESENTATION:

4   The COMPOSITE DESCRIPTION.

5   COMPOSITE TOTAL RETURNS according to one of the following:

a One-, three-, and five-year annualized COMPOSITE returns through the most recent period with the period-end date clearly identified. If the COMPOSITE has been in existence for less than five years, FIRMS MUST also present the annualized returns since the COMPOSITE INCEPTION DATE. (For example, if a COMPOSITE has been in existence for four years, FIRMS MUST present one-, three-, and four-year annualized returns through the most recent period.) Returns for periods of less than one year MUST NOT be annualized.

b Period-to-date COMPOSITE returns in addition to one-, three-, and five-year annualized COMPOSITE returns through the same period of time as presented in the corresponding COMPLIANT PRESENTATION with the period end date clearly identified. If the COMPOSITE has been in existence for less than five years, FIRMS MUST also present the annualized returns since the COMPOSITE INCEPTION DATE (For example, if a COMPOSITE has been in existence for four years, FIRMS MUST present one-, three-, and four-year annualized returns in addition to the period-to-date COMPOSITE return.) Returns for periods of less than one year MUST NOT be annualized.

c Period-to-date COMPOSITE returns in addition to five years of annual COMPOSITE returns (or for each annual period since the COMPOSITE INCEPTION DATE if the COMPOSITE has been in existence for less than five years) with the period end date clearly identified. The annual returns MUST be calculated through the same period of time as presented in the corresponding COMPLIANT PRESENTATION.

6 Whether returns are presented GROSS-OF-FEES and/or NET-OF-FEES.

7 The TOTAL RETURN for the BENCHMARK for the same periods for which the COMPOSITE return is presented. FIRMS MUST present TOTAL RETURNS for the same BENCHMARK as presented in the corresponding COMPLIANT PRESENTATION.

8 The BENCHMARK DESCRIPTION.

9 If the FIRM determines no appropriate BENCHMARK for the COMPOSITE exists, the FIRM MUST disclose why no BENCHMARK is presented.

10 The currency used to express performance.

11 The presence, use, and extent of leverage, derivatives, and short positions, if material, including a description of the frequency of use and characteristics of the instruments sufficient to identify risks.

12 For any performance presented in an advertisement for periods prior to 1 January 2000 that does not comply with the GIPS standards, FIRMS MUST disclose the periods of non-compliance.

13 If the advertisement conforms with laws and/or regulations that conflict with the REQUIREMENTS of the GIPS standards and/or the GIPS Advertising Guidelines, FIRMS MUST disclose this fact and disclose the manner in which the laws and/or regulations conflict with the GIPS standards and/or the GIPS Advertising Guidelines.

IV. VERIFICATION

VERIFICATION is intended to provide a FIRM and its existing clients and PROSPECTIVE CLIENTS additional confidence in the FIRM's claim of compliance with the GIPS standards. VERIFICATION may increase the knowledge of the FIRM's performance measurement team and improve the consistency and quality of the FIRM's COMPLIANT PRESENTATIONS. VERIFICATION may also provide improved internal processes and procedures as well as marketing advantages to the FIRM. Verification does not ensure the accuracy of any specific COMPOSITE presentation.

The GIPS standards RECOMMEND that FIRMS be verified. VERIFICATION brings additional credibility to the claim of compliance and supports the overall guiding principles of fair representation and full disclosure of a FIRM's investment performance.

The VERIFICATION procedures attempt to strike a balance between ensuring the quality, accuracy, and relevance of performance presentations and minimizing the cost to FIRMS.

Scope and Purpose of Verification

1   VERIFICATION MUST be performed by a qualified independent third party.

2   VERIFICATION assesses whether:

   a   The FIRM has complied with all the COMPOSITE construction REQUIREMENTS of the GIPS standards on a FIRM-wide basis and

   b   The FIRM's policies and procedures are designed to calculate and present performance in compliance with the GIPS standards.

3   A single VERIFICATION REPORT is issued with respect to the whole FIRM. VERIFICATION cannot be carried out on a COMPOSITE and, accordingly, does not provide assurance about the performance of any specific COMPOSITE. Firms MUST NOT state that a particular COMPOSITE has been "verified" or make any claim to that effect.

4   The initial minimum period for which VERIFICATION can be performed is one year (or from FIRM inception date through period end if less than one year) of a FIRM's presented performance. The RECOMMENDED period over which VERIFICATION is performed is that part of the FIRM's performance for which compliance with the GIPS standards is claimed.

5   A VERIFICATION REPORT MUST opine that:

   a   The FIRM has complied with all the COMPOSITE construction REQUIREMENTS of the GIPS standards on a FIRM-wide basis, and

   b   The FIRM's policies and procedures are designed to calculate and present performance in compliance with the GIPS standards.

   The FIRM MUST NOT state that it has been verified unless a VERIFICATION REPORT has been issued.

6   A principal verifier may accept the work of another verifier as part of the basis for the principal verifier's opinion. A principal verifier may also choose to rely on the audit and/or internal control work of a qualified and reputable independent third party. In addition, a principal verifier may choose to rely on the other audit and/or internal control work performed by the VERIFICATION firm. If reliance on another party's work is planned, the scope of work, including time period covered, results of procedures performed, qualifications, competency, objectivity, and reputation of the other party, MUST be assessed by the principal verifier when making the determination as to whether to place any reliance on such work. Reliance considerations and conclusions MUST be documented by the principal verifier. The principal verifier MUST use professional skepticism when deciding whether to place reliance on work performed by another independent third party.

7   Sample PORTFOLIO Selection: Verifiers MUST subject the entire FIRM to testing when performing VERIFICATION procedures unless reliance is placed on work performed by a qualified and reputable independent third party or appropriate alternative control procedures have been performed by the verifier. Verifiers may use a sampling methodology when performing such procedures. Verifiers MUST consider the following criteria when selecting samples:

   a   Number of COMPOSITES at the FIRM;

   b   Number of PORTFOLIOS in each COMPOSITE;

   c   Type of COMPOSITE;

d TOTAL FIRM ASSETS;

e Internal control structure at the FIRM (system of checks and balances in place);

f Number of years being verified; and

g Computer applications, software used in the construction and maintenance of COMPOSITES, the use of external performance measurers, and the method of calculating performance.

This list is not all-inclusive and contains only the minimum criteria that MUST be considered in the selection and evaluation of a sample. For example, one potentially useful approach would be to include in the sample a PORTFOLIO that has the largest impact on COMPOSITE performance because of its size or because of extremely good or bad performance. Missing or incomplete documents, or the presence of errors, would normally be expected to warrant selecting a larger sample or applying additional VERIFICATION procedures.

8 After performing the VERIFICATION, the verifier may conclude that the FIRM is not in compliance with the GIPS standards or that the records of the FIRM cannot support a VERIFICATION. In such situations, the verifier MUST issue a statement to the FIRM clarifying why a VERIFICATION REPORT could not be issued. A VERIFICATION REPORT MUST NOT be issued when the verifier knows that the FIRM is not in compliance with the GIPS standards or the records of the FIRM cannot support a VERIFICATION.

9 The minimum VERIFICATION procedures are described below in Section B. The VERIFICATION REPORT MUST state that the VERIFICATION has been conducted in accordance with these VERIFICATION procedures.

Required Verification Procedures

The following are the minimum procedures that verifiers MUST follow when conducting a VERIFICATION. Verifiers MUST complete the VERIFICATION in accordance with these procedures prior to issuing a VERIFICATION REPORT to the FIRM:

1 Pre-VERIFICATION Procedures:

a Knowledge of the GIPS Standards: Verifiers MUST understand all the REQUIREMENTS and RECOMMENDATIONS of the GIPS standards, including any updates, Guidance Statements, interpretations, Questions & Answers (Q&As), and clarifications published by CFA Institute and the GIPS Executive Committee, which are available on the GIPS standards website (www.gipsstandards.org) as well as in the *GIPS Handbook*.

b Knowledge of Regulations: Verifiers MUST be knowledgeable of applicable laws and regulations regarding the calculation and presentation of performance and MUST consider any differences between these laws and regulations and the GIPS standards.

c Knowledge of the FIRM: Verifiers MUST gain an understanding of the FIRM, including the corporate structure of the FIRM and how it operates.

d Knowledge of the FIRM's Policies and Procedures: Verifiers MUST understand the FIRM's policies and procedures for establishing and maintaining compliance with all the applicable REQUIREMENTS and adopted RECOMMENDATIONS of the GIPS standards. The verifier MUST obtain a copy of the FIRM's policies and procedures used in establishing and maintaining compliance with the GIPS standards and ensure that all applicable policies and procedures are properly included and adequately documented.

e Knowledge of Valuation Basis and Performance Calculations: Verifiers MUST understand the policies, procedures, and methodologies used to value PORTFOLIOS and compute investment performance.

2 VERIFICATION Procedures:

a Fundamentals of Compliance: Verifiers MUST perform sufficient procedures to determine that:

i. The FIRM is, and has been, appropriately defined;

ii. The FIRM has defined and maintained COMPOSITES in compliance with the GIPS standards;

iii. All the FIRM's actual, fee-paying, discretionary PORTFOLIOS are included in at least one COMPOSITE;

iv. The FIRM's definition of discretion has been consistently applied over time;

v. At all times, all PORTFOLIOS are included in their respective COMPOSITES and no PORTFOLIOS that belong in a particular COMPOSITE have been excluded;

vi. The FIRM's policies and procedures for ensuring the existence and ownership of client assets are appropriate and have been consistently applied;

     vii. The COMPOSITE BENCHMARK reflects the investment mandate, objective, or strategy of the COMPOSITE;

    viii. The FIRM's policies and procedures for creating and maintaining COMPOSITES have been consistently applied;

    ix. The FIRM's list of COMPOSITE DESCRIPTIONS is complete; and

    x. TOTAL FIRM ASSETS are appropriately calculated and disclosed.

b Determination of Discretionary Status of PORTFOLIOS: Verifiers MUST obtain a list of all PORTFOLIOS. Verifiers MUST select PORTFOLIOS from this list and perform sufficient procedures to determine that the FIRM's classification of the PORTFOLIOS as discretionary or non-discretionary is appropriate by referring to the PORTFOLIO's investment management agreement and/or investment guidelines and the FIRM's policies and procedures for determining investment discretion.

c Allocation of PORTFOLIOS to COMPOSITES: Verifiers MUST obtain lists of all open (both new and existing) and closed PORTFOLIOS for all COMPOSITES for the periods being verified. Verifiers MUST select PORTFOLIOS from these lists and perform sufficient procedures to determine that:

    i. The timing of inclusion in the COMPOSITE is in accordance with policies and procedures of the FIRM.

    ii. The timing of exclusion from the COMPOSITE is in accordance with policies and procedures of the FIRM.

    iii. The PORTFOLIO's investment mandate, objective, or strategy, as indicated by the PORTFOLIO's investment management agreement, investment guidelines, PORTFOLIO summary, and/or other appropriate documentation, is consistent with the COMPOSITE DEFINITION.

    iv. PORTFOLIOS are completely and accurately included in COMPOSITES by tracing selected PORTFOLIOS from:

        a The PORTFOLIO's investment management agreement and/or investment management guidelines to the COMPOSITE(s); and

        b The COMPOSITE(s) to the PORTFOLIO's investment management agreement and/or investment guidelines.

    v. PORTFOLIOS sharing the same investment mandate, objective, or strategy are included in the same COMPOSITE.

    vi. Movements from one COMPOSITE to another are appropriate and consistent with documented changes to a PORTFOLIO's investment mandate, objective, or strategy or the redefinition of the COMPOSITE.

d Data Review: For selected PORTFOLIOS, verifiers MUST perform sufficient procedures to determine that the treatment of the following items is consistent with the FIRM's policy:

    i. Classification of PORTFOLIO flows (e.g., receipts, disbursements, dividends, interest, fees, and taxes);

    ii. Accounting treatment of income, interest, and dividend accruals and receipts;

    iii. Accounting treatment of taxes, tax reclaims, and tax accruals;

    iv. Accounting treatment of purchases, sales, and the opening and closing of other positions; and

    v. Accounting treatment and valuation methodologies for investments, including derivatives.

e Performance Measurement Calculation: Recognizing that VERIFICATION does not provide assurance that specific COMPOSITE returns are correctly calculated and presented, verifiers MUST determine that the FIRM has calculated and presented performance in accordance with the FIRM's policies and procedures. Verifiers MUST perform the following procedures:

    i. Recalculate rates of return for a sample of PORTFOLIOS, determine that an acceptable return formula as REQUIRED by the GIPS standards is used, and determine that the FIRM's calculations are in accordance with the FIRM's policies and procedures. The verifier MUST also determine that any fees and expenses are treated in accordance with the GIPS standards and the FIRM's policies and procedures.

    ii. Take a sample of COMPOSITE and BENCHMARK calculations to determine the accuracy of all required numerical data (e.g., risk measures, INTERNAL DISPERSION).

    iii. If a custom BENCHMARK or combination of multiple BENCHMARKS is used, take a sample of the BENCHMARK data used by the FIRM to determine that the calculation methodology has been correctly applied and the data used are consistent with the BENCHMARK disclosure in the COMPLIANT PRESENTATION.

f   COMPLIANT PRESENTATIONS: Verifiers MUST perform sufficient procedures on a sample of COMPLIANT PRESENTATIONS to determine that the presentations include all the information and disclosures REQUIRED by the GIPS standards. The information and disclosures MUST be consistent with the FIRM's records, the FIRM's documented policies and procedures, and the results of the verifier's procedures.

g   Maintenance of Records: The verifier MUST maintain sufficient documentation to support all procedures performed supporting the issuance of the VERIFICATION REPORT, including all significant judgments and conclusions made by the verifier.

h   Representation Letter: The verifier MUST obtain a representation letter from the FIRM confirming that policies and procedures used in establishing and maintaining compliance with the GIPS standards are as described in the FIRM's policies and procedures documents and have been consistently applied throughout the periods being verified. The representation letter MUST confirm that the FIRM complies with the GIPS standards for the period being verified. The representation letter MUST also contain any other specific representations made to the verifier during the VERIFICATION.

Performance Examinations

In addition to a VERIFICATION, a FIRM may choose to have a specifically focused PERFORMANCE EXAMINATION of a particular COMPOSITE COMPLIANT PRESENTATION. However, a PERFORMANCE EXAMINATION REPORT MUST NOT be issued unless a VERIFICATION REPORT has also been issued. The PERFORMANCE EXAMINATION may be performed concurrently with the VERIFICATION.

A PERFORMANCE EXAMINATION is not REQUIRED for a FIRM to be verified. The FIRM MUST NOT state that a COMPOSITE has been examined unless the PERFORMANCE EXAMINATION REPORT has been issued for the specific COMPOSITE.

Please see the Guidance Statement on PERFORMANCE EXAMINATIONS for additional guidance.

V. GIPS GLOSSARY

ACCRUAL ACCOUNTING	The recording of financial transactions as they come into existence rather than when they are paid or settled.
ADDITIONAL INFORMATION	Information that is REQUIRED or RECOMMENDED under the GIPS standards and is not considered SUPPLEMENTAL INFORMATION.
ADMINISTRATIVE FEE	All fees other than TRADING EXPENSES and the INVESTMENT MANAGEMENT FEE. ADMINISTRATIVE FEES include CUSTODY FEES, accounting fees, auditing fees, consulting fees, legal fees, performance measurement fees, and other related fees. (See "BUNDLED FEE")
ALL-IN FEE	A type of BUNDLED FEE that can include any combination of INVESTMENT MANAGEMENT FEES, TRADING EXPENSES, CUSTODY FEES, and ADMINISTRATIVE FEES. ALL-IN-FEES are client specific and typically offered in certain jurisdictions where asset management, brokerage, and custody services are offered by the same company.
BENCHMARK	A point of reference against which the COMPOSITE's performance and/or risk is compared.
BENCHMARK DESCRIPTION	General information regarding the investments, structure, and/or characteristics of the BENCHMARK. The description MUST include the key features of the BENCHMARK or the name of the BENCHMARK for a readily recognized index or other point of reference.
BUNDLED FEE	A fee that combines multiple fees into one total or "bundled" fee. BUNDLED FEES can include any combination of INVESTMENT MANAGEMENT FEES, TRADING EXPENSES, CUSTODY FEES, and/or ADMINISTRATIVE FEES. Two examples of BUNDLED FEES are WRAP FEES and ALL-IN-FEES.
CAPITAL EMPLOYED (real estate)	The denominator of the return calculations and is defined as the "weighted-average equity" (weighted-average capital) during the measurement period. CAPITAL EMPLOYED does not include any INCOME RETURN or CAPITAL RETURN earned during the measurement period. Beginning capital is adjusted by weighting the EXTERNAL CASH FLOWS that occurred during the period.
CAPITAL RETURN (real estate)	The change in value of the REAL ESTATE investments and cash and/or cash equivalent assets held throughout the measurement period, adjusted for all capital expenditures (subtracted) and net proceeds from sales (added). The CAPITAL RETURN is computed as a percentage of the CAPITAL EMPLOYED. Also known as "capital appreciation return" or "appreciation return."
CARRIED INTEREST (real estate and private equity)	The profits that GENERAL PARTNERS are allocated from the profits on the investments made by the investment vehicle. Also known as "carry" or "promote."
CARVE-OUT	A portion of a PORTFOLIO that is by itself representative of a distinct investment strategy. It is used to create a track record for a narrower mandate from a multiple-strategy PORTFOLIO managed to a broader mandate. For periods beginning on or after 1 January 2010, a CARVE-OUT MUST be managed separately with its own cash balance.

(continued)

CLOSED-END FUND (real estate and private equity)	A type of investment vehicle where the number of investors, total COMMITTED CAPITAL, and life are fixed and not open for subscriptions and/or redemptions. CLOSED-END FUNDS have a capital call (drawdown) process in place that is controlled by the GENERAL PARTNER.
COMMITTED CAPITAL (real estate and private equity)	Pledges of capital to an investment vehicle by investors (LIMITED PARTNERS and the GENERAL PARTNER) or by the FIRM. COMMITTED CAPITAL is typically not drawn down at once but drawn down over a period of time. Also known as "commitments."
COMPLIANT PRESENTATION	A presentation for a COMPOSITE that contains all the information REQUIRED by the GIPS standards and may also include ADDITIONAL INFORMATION or SUPPLEMENTAL INFORMATION. (See Sample COMPLIANT PRESENTATIONS in Appendix A)
COMPOSITE	An aggregation of one or more PORTFOLIOS managed according to a similar investment mandate, objective, or strategy.
COMPOSITE CREATION DATE	The date when the FIRM first groups one or more PORTFOLIOS to create a COMPOSITE. The COMPOSITE CREATION DATE is not necessarily the same as the COMPOSITE INCEPTION DATE.
COMPOSITE DEFINITION	Detailed criteria that determine the assignment of PORTFOLIOS to COMPOSITES. Criteria may include investment mandate, style or strategy, asset class, the use of derivatives, leverage and/or hedging, targeted risk metrics, investment constraints or restrictions, and/or PORTFOLIO type (e.g., segregated or pooled, taxable versus tax exempt.)
COMPOSITE DESCRIPTION	General information regarding the investment mandate, objective, or strategy of the COMPOSITE. The COMPOSITE DESCRIPTION may be more abbreviated than the COMPOSITE DEFINITION but MUST include all key features of the COMPOSITE and MUST include enough information to allow a PROSPECTIVE CLIENT to understand the key characteristics of the COMPOSITE's investment mandate, objective, or strategy. (See the Sample List of Composite Descriptions in Appendix C)
COMPOSITE INCEPTION DATE	The initial date of the COMPOSITE's performance record. The COMPOSITE INCEPTION DATE is not necessarily the same as the COMPOSITE CREATION DATE.
COMPOSITE TERMINATION DATE	The date that the last PORTFOLIO exits a COMPOSITE.
CUSTODY FEE	The fees payable to the custodian for the safekeeping of PORTFOLIO assets. CUSTODY FEES are considered to be ADMINISTRATIVE FEES and typically contain an asset-based portion and a transaction-based portion. The CUSTODY FEE may also include charges for additional services, including accounting, securities lending, and/or performance measurement. Custodial fees that are charged per transaction SHOULD be included in the CUSTODY FEE and not included as part of TRADING EXPENSES.
DIRECT INVESTMENTS (private equity)	Investments made directly in PRIVATE EQUITY investments rather than investments made in fund investment vehicles or cash and/or cash equivalents.

DISTINCT BUSINESS ENTITY	A unit, division, department, or office that is organizationally and functionally segregated from other units, divisions, departments, or offices and that retains discretion over the assets it manages and that should have autonomy over the investment decision-making process. Possible criteria that can be used to determine this include: ■ being a legal entity, ■ having a distinct market or client type (e.g., institutional, retail, private client, etc.), and ■ using a separate and distinct investment process.
DISTRIBUTION (real estate and private equity)	Cash or stock distributed to LIMITED PARTNERS (or investors) from an investment vehicle. DISTRIBUTIONS are typically at the discretion of the GENERAL PARTNER (or the FIRM). DISTRIBUTIONS include both recallable and non-recallable DISTRIBUTIONS.
DPI (real estate and private equity)	SINCE INCEPTION DISTRIBUTIONS divided by SINCE INCEPTION PAID-IN CAPITAL. (See "REALIZATION MULTIPLE")
EVERGREEN FUND (private equity)	An OPEN-END FUND that allows for on-going subscriptions and/or redemptions by investors.
EX-ANTE	Before the fact.
EX-POST	After the fact.
EXTERNAL CASH FLOW	Capital (cash or investments) that enters or exits a PORTFOLIO.
EXTERNAL VALUATION (real estate)	An assessment of value performed by an independent external third party who is a qualified, PROFESSIONALLY DESIGNATED, CERTIFIED, OR LICENSED COMMERCIAL PROPERTY VALUER/APPRAISER.
FAIR VALUE	The amount at which an investment could be exchanged in a current arm's length transaction between willing parties in which the parties each act knowledgeably and prudently. The valuation MUST be determined using the objective, observable, unadjusted quoted market price for an identical investment in an active market on the measurement date, if available. In the absence of an objective, observable, unadjusted quoted market price for an identical investment in an active market on the measurement date, the valuation MUST represent the FIRM'S best estimate of the MARKET VALUE. FAIR VALUE MUST include accrued income.
FEE SCHEDULE	The FIRM'S current schedule of INVESTMENT MANAGEMENT FEES or BUNDLED FEES relevant to the particular COMPLIANT PRESENTATION.
FINAL LIQUIDATION DATE (real estate and private equity)	The date when the last PORTFOLIO in a COMPOSITE is fully distributed.
FIRM	The entity defined for compliance with the GIPS standards. (See "DISTINCT BUSINESS ENTITY")
FUND OF FUNDS (private equity)	An investment vehicle that invests in underlying investment vehicles. PRIVATE EQUITY FUNDS OF FUNDS predominately invest in CLOSED-END FUNDS and may make opportunistic DIRECT INVESTMENTS.
GENERAL PARTNER (real estate and private equity)	A class of partner in a LIMITED PARTNERSHIP. The GENERAL PARTNER (GP) retains liability for the actions of the LIMITED PARTNERSHIP. The GENERAL PARTNER is typically the fund manager, and the LIMITED PARTNERS (LPs) are the other investors in the LIMITED PARTNERSHIP. The GENERAL PARTNER earns an INVESTMENT MANAGEMENT FEE that typically includes a percentage of the LIMITED PARTNERSHIP'S profits. (See "CARRIED INTEREST")

(continued)

GROSS-OF-FEES	The return on investments reduced by any TRADING EXPENSES incurred during the period.
GROSS-OF-FEES (real estate and private equity)	The return on investments reduced by any TRANSACTION EXPENSES incurred during the period.
INCOME RETURN (real estate)	The investment income earned on all investments (including cash and cash equivalents) during the measurement period net of all non-recoverable expenditures, interest expense on debt, and property taxes. The INCOME RETURN is computed as a percentage of the CAPITAL EMPLOYED.
INTERNAL DISPERSION	A measure of the spread of the annual returns of individual PORT-FOLIOS within a COMPOSITE. Measures may include, but are not limited to, high/low, range, or STANDARD DEVIATION (asset weighted or equal weighted) of PORTFOLIO returns.
INTERNAL VALUATION (real estate)	A FIRM's best estimate of value based on the most current and accurate information available under the circumstances. INTERNAL VALUATION methodologies include applying a discounted cash flow model, using a sales comparison or replacement cost approach, or conducting a review of all significant events (both general market and asset specific) that could have a material impact on the investment.
INVESTMENT MANAGEMENT FEE	A fee payable to the FIRM for the management of a PORTFOLIO. INVESTMENT MANAGEMENT FEES are typically asset based (percentage of assets), performance based (see "PERFORMANCE-BASED FEE"), or a combination of the two but may take different forms as well. INVESTMENT MANAGEMENT FEES also include CARRIED INTEREST.
INVESTMENT MULTIPLE (TVPI) (real estate and private equity)	TOTAL VALUE divided by SINCE INCEPTION PAID-IN CAPITAL.
LARGE CASH FLOW	The level at which the FIRM determines that an EXTERNAL CASH FLOW may distort performance if the PORTFOLIO is not valued. FIRMS MUST define the amount in terms of the value of cash/asset flow or in terms of a percentage of the PORTFOLIO assets or the COMPOSITE assets.
LIMITED PARTNER (real estate and private equity)	An investor in a LIMITED PARTNERSHIP. The GENERAL PARTNER is liable for the actions of the LIMITED PARTNERSHIP, and the LIMITED PARTNERS are generally protected from legal actions and any losses beyond their COMMITTED CAPITAL.
LIMITED PARTNERSHIP (real estate and private equity)	The legal structure used by most PRIVATE EQUITY and REAL ESTATE CLOSED-END FUNDS. LIMITED PARTNERSHIPS are usually fixed life investment vehicles. The GENERAL PARTNER manages the LIMITED PARTNERSHIP pursuant to the partnership agreement.
LINK	**1** *Mathematical Linking*: The method by which sub-period returns are geometrically combined to calculate the period return using the following formula: Period return = $[(1 + R_1) \times (1 + R_2) \dots (1 + R_n)] - 1$, where $R_1, R_2 \dots R_n$ are the sub-period returns for sub-period 1 through n, respectively. **2** *Presentational Linking*: To be visually connected or otherwise associated within a COMPLIANT PRESENTATION (e.g., two pieces of information are LINKED by placing them next to each other).
MARKET VALUE	The price at which investors can buy or sell an investment at a given time multiplied by the quantity held plus any accrued income.

MUST	A provision, task, or action that is mandatory or REQUIRED to be followed or performed. (See "REQUIRE/REQUIREMENT")
MUST NOT	A task or action that is forbidden or prohibited.
NET-OF-FEES	The GROSS-OF-FEES return reduced by INVESTMENT MANAGEMENT FEES (including PERFORMANCE-BASED FEES and CARRIED INTEREST).
OPEN-END FUND (real estate and private equity)	A type of investment vehicle where the number of investors and the total COMMITTED CAPITAL is not fixed and is open for subscriptions and/or redemptions. (See "EVERGREEN FUND")
PAID-IN CAPITAL (real estate and private equity)	Capital inflows to an investment vehicle. COMMITTED CAPITAL is typically drawn down from LIMITED PARTNERS (or investors) over a period of time through a series of capital calls, which are at the discretion of the GENERAL PARTNER or FIRM. PAID-IN CAPITAL is equal to the amount of COMMITTED CAPITAL that has been drawn down SINCE INCEPTION. PAID-IN CAPITAL includes DISTRIBUTIONS that are subsequently recalled by the GENERAL PARTNER or FIRM and reinvested into the investment vehicle.
PERFORMANCE-BASED FEE	A type of INVESTMENT MANAGEMENT FEE that is typically based on the performance of the PORTFOLIO on an absolute basis or relative to a BENCHMARK.
PERFORMANCE EXAMINATION	A detailed examination of a specific COMPOSITE'S COMPLIANT PRESENTATION by an independent verifier.
PERFORMANCE EXAMINATION REPORT	A PERFORMANCE EXAMINATION REPORT is issued after a PERFORMANCE EXAMINATION has been performed and opines that a particular COMPOSITE'S COMPLIANT PRESENTATION has been prepared and presented in compliance with the GIPS standards.
PERIODICITY	The length of the time period over which a variable is measured (e.g., a variable that is measured at a monthly PERIODICITY consists of observations for each month).
PIC MULTIPLE (real estate and private equity)	SINCE INCEPTION PAID-IN CAPITAL divided by cumulative COMMITTED CAPITAL.
PORTFOLIO	An individually managed group of investments. A PORTFOLIO may be an account or pooled investment vehicle.
PRIMARY FUND (private equity)	An investment vehicle that makes DIRECT INVESTMENTS rather than investing in other investment vehicles.
PRIVATE EQUITY	Investment strategies include, but are not limited to, venture capital, leveraged buyouts, consolidations, mezzanine and distressed debt investments, and a variety of hybrids, such as venture leasing and venture factoring.
PROFESSIONALLY DESIGNATED, CERTIFIED, OR LICENSED COMMERCIAL PROPERTY VALUER/APPRAISER (real estate)	In Europe, Canada, and parts of Southeast Asia, the predominant professional designation is that of the Royal Institution of Chartered Surveyors (RICS). In the United States, the professional designation is Member [of the] Appraisal Institute (MAI). In addition, each state regulates REAL ESTATE appraisers and registers, licenses, or certifies them based on their experience and test results.
PROPRIETARY ASSETS	Investments owned by the FIRM, the FIRM'S management, and/or the FIRM'S parent company that are managed by the FIRM.

(continued)

PROSPECTIVE CLIENT	Any person or entity that has expressed interest in one of the FIRM's COMPOSITE strategies and qualifies to invest in the COMPOSITE. Existing clients may also qualify as PROSPECTIVE CLIENTS for any strategy that is different from their current investment strategy. Investment consultants and other third parties are included as PROSPECTIVE CLIENTS if they represent investors that qualify as PROSPECTIVE CLIENTS.
PUBLIC MARKET EQUIVALENT (PME) (private equity)	The performance of a public market index expressed in terms of an internal rate of return (IRR), using the same cash flows and timing as those of the COMPOSITE over the same time period. A PME can be used as a BENCHMARK by comparing the IRR of a PRIVATE EQUITY COMPOSITE with the PME of a public market index.
REAL ESTATE	Investments in:

- wholly owned or partially owned properties;
- commingled funds, property unit trusts, and insurance company separate accounts;
- unlisted, private placement securities issued by private REAL ESTATE investment trusts (REITs) and REAL ESTATE operating companies (REOCs); and
- equity-oriented debt (e.g., participating mortgage loans) or any private interest in a property where some portion of return to the investor at the time of investment is related to the performance of the underlying REAL ESTATE.

REALIZATION MULTIPLE (DPI) (real estate and private equity)	SINCE INCEPTION DISTRIBUTIONS divided by SINCE INCEPTION PAID-IN CAPITAL.
RECOMMEND/RECOMMENDATION	A suggested provision, task, or action that SHOULD be followed or performed. A RECOMMENDATION is considered to be best practice but is not a REQUIREMENT. (See "SHOULD")
REQUIRE/REQUIREMENT	A provision, task, or action that MUST be followed or performed. (See "MUST")
RESIDUAL VALUE (private equity and real estate)	The remaining equity that LIMITED PARTNERS (or investors) have in an investment vehicle at the end of the performance reporting period.
RVPI (real estate and private equity)	RESIDUAL VALUE divided by SINCE INCEPTION PAID-IN CAPITAL. (See "UNREALIZED MULTIPLE")
SECONDARY FUND (private equity)	An investment vehicle that buys interests in existing investment vehicles.
SETTLEMENT DATE ACCOUNTING	Recognizing the asset or liability on the date when the exchange of cash and investments is completed.
SHOULD	A provision, task, or action that is RECOMMENDED to be followed or performed and is considered to be best practice but is not REQUIRED. (See "RECOMMEND/RECOMMENDATION")
SIGNIFICANT CASH FLOW	The level at which the FIRM determines that a client-directed EXTERNAL CASH FLOW may temporarily prevent the FIRM from implementing the COMPOSITE strategy. The measure of significance MUST be determined as either a specific monetary amount (e.g., €50,000,000) or a percentage of PORTFOLIO assets (based on the most recent valuation).
SINCE INCEPTION (real estate and private equity)	From the initial cash flow of a COMPOSITE.

SINCE INCEPTION INTERNAL RATE OF RETURN (SI-IRR) (real estate and private equity)	The internal rate of return (IRR) is the implied discount rate or effective compounded rate of return that equates the present value of cash outflows with the present value of cash inflows. The SI-IRR is a special case of the IRR that equates the present value of all cash flows (capital calls and DISTRIBUTIONS) with the period end value. The SI-IRR is always annualized except when the reporting period is less than one year, in which case the SI-IRR is not annualized.
STANDARD DEVIATION	A measure of the variability of returns. As a measure of INTERNAL DISPERSION, STANDARD DEVIATION quantifies the distribution of the returns of the individual PORTFOLIOS within the COMPOSITE. As a measure of historical risk, STANDARD DEVIATION quantifies the variability of the COMPOSITE and/or BENCHMARK returns over time. Also referred to as "external STANDARD DEVIATION."
SUB-ADVISOR	A third-party investment manager hired by the FIRM to manage some or all of the assets for which a FIRM has investment management responsibility.
SUPPLEMENTAL INFORMATION	Any performance-related information included as part of a COMPLIANT PRESENTATION that supplements or enhances the REQUIRED and/or RECOMMENDED provisions of the GIPS standards.
TEMPORARY NEW ACCOUNT	An account for temporarily holding client-directed EXTERNAL CASH FLOWS until they are invested according to the COMPOSITE strategy or disbursed. FIRMS can use a TEMPORARY NEW ACCOUNT to remove the effect of a SIGNIFICANT CASH FLOW on a PORTFOLIO. When a SIGNIFICANT CASH FLOW occurs in a PORTFOLIO, the FIRM may direct the EXTERNAL CASH FLOW to a TEMPORARY NEW ACCOUNT according to the COMPOSITE'S SIGNIFICANT CASH FLOW policy.
TIME-WEIGHTED RATE OF RETURN	A method of calculating period-by-period returns that negates the effects of EXTERNAL CASH FLOWS.
TOTAL FIRM ASSETS	All discretionary and non-discretionary assets for which a FIRM has investment management responsibility. TOTAL FIRM ASSETS includes assets assigned to a SUB-ADVISOR provided the FIRM has discretion over the selection of the SUB-ADVISOR.
TOTAL RETURN	The rate of return that includes the realized and unrealized gains and losses plus income for the measurement period.
TOTAL RETURN (real estate)	The rate of return, including all CAPITAL RETURN and INCOME RETURN components, expressed as a percentage of the CAPITAL EMPLOYED over the measurement period.
TOTAL VALUE (real estate and private equity)	RESIDUAL VALUE plus DISTRIBUTIONS.
TRADE DATE ACCOUNTING	Recognizing the asset or liability on the date of the purchase or sale and not on the settlement date. Recognizing the asset or liability within three days of the date the transaction is entered into (trade date, T+1, T+2, or T+3) satisfies the TRADE DATE ACCOUNTING REQUIREMENT for purposes of the GIPS standards. (See "SETTLEMENT DATE ACCOUNTING")
TRADING EXPENSES	The actual costs of buying or selling investments. These costs typically take the form of brokerage commissions, exchange fees and/or taxes, and/or bid–offer spreads from either internal or external brokers. Custodial fees charged per transaction SHOULD be considered CUSTODY FEES and not TRADING EXPENSES.

(continued)

Transaction expenses (real estate and private equity)	All actual legal, financial, advisory, and investment banking fees related to buying, selling, restructuring, and/or recapitalizing PORTFOLIO investments as well as TRADING EXPENSES, if any.
TVPI (real estate and private equity)	TOTAL VALUE divided by SINCE INCEPTION PAID-IN CAPITAL. (See "INVESTMENT MULTIPLE")
Unrealized multiple (RVPI) (real estate and private equity)	RESIDUAL VALUE divided by SINCE INCEPTION PAID-IN CAPITAL.
Verification	A process by which an independent verifier assesses whether

1 the FIRM has complied with all the COMPOSITE construction REQUIREMENTS of the GIPS standards on a FIRM-wide basis and

2 the FIRM's policies and procedures are designed to calculate and present performance in compliance with the GIPS standards.

Verification report

A VERIFICATION REPORT is issued after a VERIFICATION has been performed and opines that the FIRM has complied with all the COMPOSITE construction REQUIREMENTS of the GIPS standards on a FIRM-wide basis and that the FIRM's policies and procedures are designed to calculate and present performance in compliance with the GIPS standards.

Vintage year
(real estate and private equity)

Two methods used to determine VINTAGE YEAR are:

1 the year of the investment vehicle's first drawdown or capital call from its investors; or

2 the year when the first COMMITTED CAPITAL from outside investors is closed and legally binding.

Wrap fee

WRAP FEES are a type of BUNDLED FEE and are specific to a particular investment product. The WRAP FEE is charged by a WRAP FEE sponsor for investment management services and typically includes associated TRADING EXPENSES that cannot be separately identified. WRAP FEES can be all-inclusive, asset-based fees and may include a combination of INVESTMENT MANAGEMENT FEES, TRADING EXPENSES, CUSTODY FEES, and/or ADMINISTRATIVE FEES. A WRAP FEE PORTFOLIO is sometimes referred to as a "separately managed account" (SMA) or "managed account."

APPENDIX A: SAMPLE COMPLIANT PRESENTATIONS

SAMPLE 1 INVESTMENT FIRM BALANCED GROWTH COMPOSITE

1 January 2002 through 31 December 2011

Year	Composite Gross Return (%)	Composite Net Return (%)	Custom Benchmark Return (%)	Composite 3-Yr St Dev (%)	Benchmark 3-Yr St Dev (%)	Number of Portfolios	Internal Dispersion (%)	Composite Assets ($ M)	Firm Assets ($ M)
2002	−10.5	−11.4	−11.8			31	4.5	165	236
2003	16.3	15.1	13.2			34	2.0	235	346
2004	7.5	6.4	8.9			38	5.7	344	529
2005	1.8	0.8	0.3			45	2.8	445	695
2006	11.2	10.1	12.2			48	3.1	520	839
2007	6.1	5.0	7.1			49	2.8	505	1,014
2008	−21.3	−22.1	−24.9			44	2.9	475	964
2009	16.5	15.3	14.7			47	3.1	493	983
2010	10.6	9.5	13.0			51	3.5	549	1,114
2011	2.7	1.7	0.4	7.1	7.4	54	2.5	575	1,236

Sample 1 Investment Firm claims compliance with the Global Investment Performance Standards (GIPS®) and has prepared and presented this report in compliance with the GIPS standards. Sample 1 Investment Firm has been independently verified for the periods 1 January 2000 through 31 December 2010. The verification report is available upon request. Verification assesses whether (1) the firm has complied with all the composite construction requirements of the GIPS standards on a firm-wide basis and (2) the firm's policies and procedures are designed to calculate and present performance in compliance with the GIPS standards. Verification does not ensure the accuracy of any specific composite presentation.

Notes:

1 Sample 1 Investment Firm is a balanced portfolio investment manager that invests solely in US-based securities. Sample 1 Investment Firm is defined as an independent investment management firm that is not affiliated with any parent organization. Policies for valuing portfolios, calculating performance, and preparing compliant presentations are available upon request.

2 The Balanced Growth Composite includes all institutional balanced portfolios that invest in large-cap US equities and investment-grade bonds with the goal of providing long-term capital growth and steady income from a well-diversified strategy. Although the strategy allows for equity exposure ranging between 50–70%, the typical allocation is between 55–65%. The account minimum for the composite is $5 million.

3 The custom benchmark is 60% YYY US Equity Index and 40% ZZZ US Aggregate Bond Index. The benchmark is rebalanced monthly.

4 Valuations are computed and performance is reported in US dollars.

5 Gross-of-fees returns are presented before management and custodial fees but after all trading expenses. Composite and benchmark returns are presented net of non-reclaimable withholding taxes. Net-of-fees returns are calculated by deducting the highest fee of 0.83% from the monthly gross composite return. The management fee schedule is as follows: 1.00% on the first $25 million; 0.60% thereafter.

6 This composite was created in February 2000. A complete list of composite descriptions is available upon request.

7   Internal dispersion is calculated using the equal-weighted standard deviation of annual gross returns of those portfolios that were included in the composite for the entire year.

8   The three-year annualized standard deviation measures the variability of the composite and the benchmark returns over the preceding 36-month period. The standard deviation is not presented for 2002 through 2010 because monthly composite and benchmark returns were not available and is not required for periods prior to 2011.

SAMPLE 2   ASSET MANAGEMENT COMPANY ACTIVE WORLD EQUITY COMPOSITE

Creation Date: 1 July 2005
Reporting Currency: EUR

Year	Gross Return (%)	XYZ World Index Return (%)	Dispersion (Range) (%)	# of Portfolios	Composite Assets (€ M)	% of Firm Assets (%)
2011	−1.9	−0.5	0.2	6	224.9	2.1
2010	16.3	13.5	0.7	8	256.7	2.0
2009	29.0	25.8	1.5	8	205.6	1.9
2008	−39.8	−36.4	1.3	7	164.1	1.5
2007	−2.8	−2.7	n/a	≤ 5	143.7	1.2
2006	9.3	7.5	n/a	≤ 5	62.8	0.4
2005*	14.2	12.6	n/a	≤ 5	16.1	< 0.1

*Returns are for the period from 1 July 2005 (inception date) through 31 December 2005.

Compliance Statement

Sample 2 Asset Management Company claims compliance with the Global Investment Performance Standards (GIPS®) and has prepared and presented this report in compliance with the GIPS standards. Sample 2 Asset Management Company has not been independently verified.

Definition of the Firm

Sample 2 Asset Management Company is an independent investment management firm that was established in 1997. Sample 2 Asset Management Company manages a variety of equity, fixed-income, and balanced assets for primarily European clients.

Policies

Sample 2 Asset Management Company's policies for valuing portfolios, calculating performance, and preparing compliant presentations are available upon request.

Composite Description

The Active World Equity Composite includes accounts whose objective is to exceed the XYZ World Index by 2% over a rolling three-year period. Securities are selected using the firm's proprietary analytics tool, which selects securities expected to be the top performers from within the XYZ World Index universe. Portfolios are more concentrated, typically holding approximately 100–120 securities, versus the benchmark, which reflects the performance of more than 500 holdings. Composite returns may, therefore, have a lower correlation with the benchmark than a more diversified global equity strategy.

Benchmark

The benchmark is the XYZ World Index, which is designed to measure the equity market performance of developed market countries. The benchmark is market-cap weighted and is composed of all XYZ country-specific developed market indices. Sources of foreign exchange rates may be different between the composite and the benchmark; however, there have not been material differences to date. Benchmark returns are net of withholding taxes.

Fees

Returns are presented gross of management fees, custodial fees, and withholding taxes but net of all trading expenses.

List of Composites

A list of all composite descriptions is available upon request.

Fee Schedule

The standard fixed management fee for accounts with assets under management of up to €50 million is 0.35% per annum; 0.25% thereafter.

Minimum Account Size

The minimum portfolio size for inclusion in the composite is €1 million.

Internal Dispersion

Internal dispersion is calculated using the asset-weighted standard deviation of annual gross-of-fees returns of those portfolios that were included in the composite for the entire year. For those years when less than six portfolios were included in the composite for the full year, no dispersion measure is presented.

Ex-Post Standard Deviation

The three-year annualized ex-post standard deviation of the composite and benchmark as of each year end is as follows:

Year	Composite 3-Yr St Dev (%)	Benchmark 3-Yr St Dev (%)
2011	12.9	14.6
2010	13.2	14.1
2009	17.0	16.3
2008	15.6	14.2

SAMPLE 3   REAL ESTATE: OPEN-END FUNDS/SEPARATE ACCOUNTS

Real Estate Advisors Value-Added Strategy Composite
Schedule of Performance Results 1 January 2002 through 31 December 2011

Year	Composite Gross-of-Fees Returns					Composite Net-of-Fees Returns	Value-Added Benchmark Returns (Open-End Funds/ Separate Accounts)			Composite Statistics at Year End				
	Income Return (%)	Capital Return (%)	Total Return (%)	Low (%)	High (%)	Total Return (%)	Income Return (%)	Capital Return (%)	Total Return (%)	# of Portfolios	Composite Assets (HKD Million)	External Appraisal % of Composite Assets	Total Firm Assets (HKD Million)	Non-Real Estate % of Composite Assets
2002	7.9	1.9	9.9	n/a	n/a	8.8	8.4	−1.6	7.1	≤ 5	3,085	25	13,919	0
2003	8.5	2.9	11.7	5.8	20.4	10.5	8.0	1.0	9.2	6	3,294	25	14,911	0
2004	8.2	2.6	10.9	5.5	19.2	8.3	7.5	6.7	14.4	7	3,348	44	15,144	0
2005	6.6	11.2	18.1	9.0	31.6	16.6	6.8	12.7	19.7	7	3,728	72	19,794	0
2006	6.1	7.9	14.2	7.1	24.9	12.5	6.2	9.9	16.3	8	4,022	46	20,482	0
2007	5.4	8.0	13.7	6.8	23.9	11.8	5.6	9.9	15.6	7	4,348	33	24,219	0
2008	5.2	−11.4	−6.6	−9.8	−1.6	−8.2	5.1	−11.1	−5.9	7	3,836	100	21,447	0
2009	7.5	2.7	10.3	5.2	18.1	7.4	7.3	3.2	10.8	7	3,371	52	16,601	0
2010	7.2	1.7	9.0	4.2	19.5	6.9	7.8	3.1	11.1	7	2,852	38	4,516	0
2011	7.2	2.8	10.2	5.1	17.8	8.1	7.1	3.2	10.6	7	3,457	50	17,414	5
Annualized Returns (%)														
3 Year	7.3	1.9	9.8			7.5	7.4	3.2	10.8					
5 Year	6.5	2.9	7.1			5.0	6.6	1.4	8.2					
7 Year	6.4	2.6	9.6			7.6	6.6	4.2	10.9					
10 Year	7.0	11.2	10.0			8.1	7.0	3.5	10.7					
Since Inception	7.0	7.9	10.0			8.1	7.0	3.5	10.7					

Disclosures

Compliance Statement

Sample 3 Real Estate Advisors claims compliance with the Global Investment Performance Standards (GIPS®) and has prepared and presented this report in compliance with the GIPS standards. Sample 3 Real Estate Advisors has been independently verified for the periods 1 January 2006 through 31 December 2011. The verification reports are available upon request.

Verification assesses whether 1) the firm has complied with all the composite construction requirements of the GIPS standards on a firm-wide basis and 2) the firm's policies and procedures are designed to calculate and present performance in compliance with the GIPS standards. Verification does not ensure the accuracy of any specific composite presentation.

The Firm

Sample 3 Real Estate Advisors (the "Firm"), a subsidiary of Sample 3 Capital, Inc., is based in Hong Kong and manages international real estate strategies. A list of the Firm's composite descriptions is available upon request.

The Composite

The Value-Added Strategy Composite consists of all discretionary open-end funds and separate accounts managed by the Firm using a value-added investment strategy with an equal income and appreciation focus and having a minimum portfolio size of HKD 10 million. Portfolio management will invest in only Asian multi-family, office, industrial, and retail property types that require correction or mitigation of the investments' operating, financial, redevelopment, and/or management risk(s). A moderate level of leverage ranging between 30% and 40% is used. Real estate investments are generally illiquid, and the investment outlook may change given the availability of credit or other financing sources.

The composite was created on 1 January 2006. The returns presented for periods prior to 2006 are not in compliance with the GIPS standards. Annual internal dispersion is presented using the high and low gross total returns for those portfolios that have been in the composite for the entire year.

Description of Discretion

The Firm has responsibility for sourcing, valuing, and managing the acquisition and disposition of assets. Although some of the Firm's separate accounts require client approval for the acquisition and disposition of assets, the Firm defines such portfolios as discretionary because its recommendations are consistent with the investment strategy and such client approvals are typically perfunctory.

Valuation

Real estate assets are internally valued by the Firm quarterly. For periods prior to 1 January 2011, assets were externally appraised by an independent appraiser at least every 36 months. Beginning 1 January 2011, assets are externally appraised annually unless client agreements stipulate otherwise, in which case such assets are appraised at least every 36 months or per the client agreement if the client agreement requires external valuation more frequently than every 36 months. The percentage of composite assets valued using an external valuation is shown for each annual period. When market circumstances dictate, the Firm may increase the frequency of external appraisals. All valuations are performed as of calendar quarter-ends.

Internal property valuations are determined by applying market discount rates to future projections of gross cash flows and capitalized terminal values over the expected holding period for each asset. To the extent leverage (debt) is used, the debt is valued separately from the real estate. Property mortgages, notes, and loans are marked to market using prevailing interest rates for comparable property loans if the terms of existing loans preclude the immediate repayment of such loans. Due to the nature of real estate investments, valuations are based upon subjective unobservable inputs.

Basis of Accounting

All funds in the composite report their assets and liabilities on a fair value basis using International Financial Reporting Standards (IFRS).

Calculation of Performance Returns

Returns are presented in Hong Kong dollars and are net of leverage. Net-of-fee returns are net of actual investment management fees including incentive fees, which are recorded on an accrual basis. Returns include cash and cash equivalents and related interest income.

Capital expenditures, tenant improvements, and lease commissions are capitalized, included in the cost of property, and reflected in the capital return component. Income and capital returns may not equal total returns due to the compounding linking of quarterly returns. Composite returns are calculated quarterly on an asset-weighted basis using beginning-of-period values. Annual returns are calculated by linking quarterly composite returns.

Policies for valuing portfolios, calculating performance, and preparing compliant presentations are available upon request.

Investment Management Fees

Some of the funds in the composite pay incentive fees ranging between 10% and 20% of profits in excess of a targeted SI-IRR. The standard annual investment management fee schedule for separately managed institutional accounts is as follows:

Up to HKD 30 million:	1.6%
HKD 30–50 million:	1.3%
Over HKD 50 million:	1.0%

Benchmark

The benchmark is the Value-Added Open-End Fund/Separate Account Index (the "Benchmark"). The Benchmark returns have been taken from published sources. The Benchmark is leveraged, includes various real estate property types, and excludes cash, cash equivalents, and other non-property-related assets, liabilities, income, and expenses. The extent of leverage used by the Benchmark may be different from that of the portfolios in the composite. As of 31 December 2011, the Benchmark leverage was 52%.

SAMPLE 4   REAL ESTATE: CLOSED-END FUND

2006 Value-Added Strategy Closed-End Fund Composite
Schedule of Performance Results 1 April 2006 through 31 December 2011

	Composite Gross TWR			Composite NET TWR	Benchmark				Composite at Year-End					
Year	Income Return (%)	Capital Return (%)	Total Return (%)	Total Return (%)	Income Return (%)	Capital Return (%)	Total Return (%)	# of Portfolios	Composite Assets (U.S. Million)	Leverage (%)	External Appraisal % of Composite Assets	Total Firm Assets (U.S. Million)	% of Firm Assets	Non-Real Estate % of Composite Assets
4/06–12/06	–3.2	0.8	–2.5	–4.0	4.9	2.2	7.2	1	70	40	35	2,641	20	0
2007	2.5	3.4	6.0	4.5	5.8	1.1	7.1	1	164	45	28	3,125	18	0
2008	6.2	1.9	8.2	6.7	6.9	3.8	10.9	1	215	50	100	2,754	18	0
2009	7.4	30.7	38.6	36.1	7.0	10.2	17.4	1	256	53	44	2,142	21	0
2010	6.6	–13.7	–7.3	–8.8	6.1	–8.8	–2.5	1	111	57	28	1,873	19	0
2011	5.8	–1.5	4.3	2.8	5.4	–2.6	3.0	1	112	60	85	2,247	20	15

Year	Gross SI-IRR	Net SI-IRR	Total Committed Capital (U.S. Million)	Paid-In Capital (U.S. Million)	Cumulative Distributions (U.S. Million)	TVPI Multiple	DPI Multiple	RVPI Multiple	PIC Multiple
4/06–12/06	–2.3	–3.1	250	71	0	0.99	0.00	0.99	0.28
2007	3.7	2.2	250	161	1	1.02	0.01	1.02	0.64
2008	5.8	4.2	250	226	26	1.07	0.12	0.95	0.90
2009	18.5	15.2	250	236	76	1.41	0.32	1.08	0.94
2010	11.5	9.8	250	240	201	1.30	0.84	0.46	0.96
2011	10.8	9.1	250	245	208	1.31	0.85	0.46	0.98

TVPI (investment multiple) = total value to paid-in capital
DPI (realization multiple) = cumulative distributions to paid-in capital
RVPI (unrealized multiple) = residual value to paid-in capital
PIC (PIC multiple) = paid-in capital to committed capital

Disclosures

Compliance Statement

Sample 4 Real Estate Managers claims compliance with the Global Investment Performance Standards (GIPS®) and has prepared and presented this report in compliance with the GIPS standards. Sample 4 Real Estate Managers has been independently verified for the periods 1 January 2006 through 31 December 2011. The verification reports are available upon request.

Verification assesses whether (1) the firm has complied with all the composite construction requirements of the GIPS standards on a firm-wide basis and (2) the firm's policies and procedures are designed to calculate and present performance in compliance with the GIPS standards. Verification does not ensure the accuracy of any specific composite presentation.

The Firm

Sample 4 Real Estate Managers (the "Firm") is a registered investment adviser under the Investment Advisers Act of 1940. A list of the Firm's composite descriptions is available upon request.

The Composite

The 2006 Value-Added Strategy Closed-End Fund Composite includes a single closed-end commingled fund managed by the Firm using a value-added investment strategy with a focus on both income and appreciation. Portfolio management intends to invest in properties located in major markets within the United States with higher operational risk than traditional property types. The target level of leverage is 50% with a maximum allowable level of 60%. Real estate investments are generally illiquid, and the investment outlook may change given the availability of credit or other financing sources. If investment opportunities and/or exit strategies become limited, the life of the fund may be extended and capital calls and distributions may be delayed. The composite was created on 1 January 2006. The composite vintage year is 2006, which was determined based on the fund's first capital call in April 2006.

Description of Discretion

The Firm has complete discretion for all investment activities within the fund.

Valuation

Real estate investments are internally valued by the Firm quarterly. For periods prior to 1 January 2011, investments were externally appraised by an independent appraiser at least every 36 months. Beginning 1 January 2011, assets are externally appraised annually. The percentage of composite assets valued using an external valuation is shown for each annual period. When market circumstances dictate, the Firm may increase the frequency of external appraisals. All valuations are performed as of calendar quarter-ends. Internal investment valuations are determined by applying market discount rates to future projections of net cash flows (gross real estate cash flows less debt service) and capitalized terminal values over the expected holding period for each asset. Due to the nature of real estate investments, valuations are based upon subjective unobservable inputs.

Basis of Accounting

All assets and liabilities are reported on a fair value basis using US Generally Accepted Accounting Principles for non-operating companies.

Calculation of Performance Returns and Metrics

Returns are presented in US dollars and are net of leverage. Net-of-fee returns are net of actual investment management fees, including incentive fees, which are recorded on an accrual basis.

Capital expenditures, tenant improvements, and lease commissions are capitalized, included in the cost of property, and reflected in the capital return component. Income and capital returns may not equal total returns due to the compounding linking of quarterly returns. Composite time-weighted returns are calculated quarterly on an asset-weighted basis using beginning-of-period values. Annual returns are calculated by linking quarterly composite returns.

SI-IRRs are calculated using quarterly cash flows through 2010 and daily cash flows starting in 2011.

Policies for valuing portfolios, calculating performance, and preparing presentations are available upon request.

Investment Management Fees

The fund pays an incentive fee of 15% of profits if the SI-IRR exceeds a preferred return to investors of 11%. The incentive fee is calculated annually. The standard annual investment management fee schedule for separately managed institutional accounts is as follows:

Up to $100 million:	1.50%
Over $100 million:	1.25%

Benchmark

The benchmark is the Value-Added Closed-End Fund Index (the "Benchmark"). The Benchmark is a time-weighted return index and returns have been taken from published sources. The Benchmark is leveraged and includes various real estate investment and property types, cash and other non-property-related assets, liabilities, income, and expenses. The extent of leverage used by the Benchmark may be different from that of the fund in the composite. As of 31 December 2011, the Benchmark leverage was 60%. There is no SI-IRR benchmark available for the 2006 vintage year.

SAMPLE 5   PRIVATE EQUITY: FUND OF FUNDS BY INVESTMENT STRATEGY

ABC Fund of Funds Manager, LLC
2006 Buyout Strategy Fund of Funds Composite
Results Reported as of Calendar Year End

Year End	# of Portfolios	Gross-of-Fees SI-IRR (%)	Net-of-Fees SI-IRR (%)	Benchmark SI-IRR (%)	Composite Assets ($ Mil)	Composite % of Firm Assets
2006*	8	26.9	26.4	17.2	2,336	80.8
2007	10	18.5	17.8	10.2	2,512	83.6
2008	11	18.7	18.1	11.0	3,227	84.2
2009	13	19.6	18.9	11.5	4,518	84.8
2010	13	20.7	20.1	11.8	6,330	85.2
2011	13	21.9	21.3	11.8	9,269	86.0
2012	14	22.2	21.7	12.3	12,286	86.4
2013	14	15.1	14.4	9.6	12,346	87.7

*Partial year from 15 April 2006 (inception) through 31 December 2006.

Year End	Paid-In Capital ($ Mil)	Cumulative Committed Capital ($ Mil)	Since Inception Distributions	Investment Multiple (TVPI)	Realization Multiple (DPI)	Unrealized Multiple (RVPI)	PIC Multiple (PIC)
2006	1,556	3,177	1,205	1.5	0.8	0.7	0.48
2007	1,908	3,675	1,341	1.3	0.7	0.6	0.51
2008	2,371	5,166	1,623	1.4	0.7	0.7	0.45
2009	3,254	6,401	2,186	1.4	0.7	0.7	0.50
2010	4,400	8,370	2,950	1.4	0.7	0.8	0.51
2011	6,303	11,344	4,138	1.5	0.7	0.8	0.54
2012	8,167	13,713	6,513	1.5	0.8	0.7	0.69
2013	9,651	15,290	7,091	1.3	0.7	0.5	0.71

Aggregate Performance of Underlying
Investments by Vintage Year
Results Reported as of 31 December 2013

Vintage Year	Gross-of-Fees Annualized SI-IRR (%)	Benchmark SI-IRR (%)
2006	22.3	2.5
2007	13.4	1.9
2008	26.0	7.1
2009	18.1	3.9
2010	0.7	1.0
2011	−16.2	−7.5

(Continued)		
Vintage Year	**Gross-of-Fees Annualized SI-IRR (%)**	**Benchmark SI-IRR (%)**
2012	−25.6	−19.9
2013	−49.9	−40.3

Vintage Year	Paid-In Capital ($ Mil)	Cumulative Committed Capital ($ Mil)	Since Inception Distributions ($ Mil)	Investment Multiple (TVPI)	Realization Multiple (DPI)	Unrealized Multiple (RVPI)	PIC Multiple (PIC)
2006	731	724	939	3.0	1.3	1.7	1.0
2007	710	234	294	1.8	0.4	1.3	3.0
2008	1,475	1,220	1,442	2.0	1.0	1.0	1.2
2009	1,640	1,048	1,156	1.9	0.7	1.2	1.6
2010	1,896	3,695	1,124	1.9	0.6	1.4	0.5
2011	1,984	4,518	1,100	2.1	0.6	1.5	0.4
2012	680	1,998	938	2.2	1.4	0.8	0.3
2013	535	1,853	100	1.1	0.2	0.9	0.3

TVPI (investment multiple) = total value to paid-in capital
DPI (realization multiple) = cumulative distributions to paid-in capital
RVPI (unrealized multiple) = residual value to paid-in capital
PIC (PIC multiple) = paid-in capital to committed capital

Compliance Statement

ABC Fund of Funds Manager, LLC, claims compliance with the Global Investment Performance Standards (GIPS®) and has prepared and presented this report in compliance with the GIPS standards. ABC Fund of Funds Manager, LLC, has been independently verified for the periods 15 April 2006 through 31 December 2012.

Verification assesses whether (1) the firm has complied with all the composite construction requirements of the GIPS standards on a firm-wide basis and (2) the firm's policies and procedures are designed to calculate and present performance in compliance with the GIPS standards. Verification does not ensure the accuracy of any specific composite presentation. The verification report is available upon request.

The Firm

ABC Fund of Funds Manager, LLC, is an independent private equity investment firm with offices in New York, London, and Tokyo. The firm's list of composite descriptions, as well as information regarding the firm's policies for valuing investments, calculating performance, and preparing compliant presentations, are available upon request.

The Composite

The 2006 Buyout Strategy Fund of Funds Composite includes primary and secondary partnership investments with strategies focused on leveraged and growth-oriented buyouts primarily in the United States. Managers of partnerships are expected to focus on reducing costs, preparing companies for downturn, and providing operational improvement rather than financial engineering. Investments may be in small, medium, and large buyout partnerships, aiming to make selective commitments diversifying across stages, industries, and vintage years. Secondary deals take advantage of distressed primary partnership sales providing access to an increased mix of assets. The underlying funds are leveraged 100–300%. Private equity investments are illiquid and, therefore, if investment opportunities and/or exit strategies become limited, the life of the fund may be extended and capital calls and distributions may be delayed. The composite was created on 31 December 2006. The vintage year is 2006 and was determined by the initial subscription date of the fund of funds.

Valuation

The firm uses valuations reported by the general partner of the investment partnerships. Given the nature of the investments, all valuations are determined using both subjective observable and subjective unobservable inputs.

Calculation of Performance Returns

The fund's SI-IRR calculation uses daily cash flows. All cash flows and values used to calculate returns are in, or have been converted to, US dollars. Gross returns are net of all underlying investment partnership expenses, management fees, and carried interest but gross of ABC Fund of Funds Manager's management fees. Net returns are net of all underlying partnership fees and expenses, including ABC Fund of Funds Manager's management fees.

Investment Management Fee

ABC Fund of Funds Manager's management fee varies based on the size of the commitment and structure of the program. The management fee is 100 basis points, based on the total commitment to a fund of funds, plus a 10% carry on total gains. Net returns are calculated using actual management fees of the fund of funds and underlying funds, including performance fees.

Benchmark

The benchmark is derived from private equity dollar-weighted IRRs, and the calculation is based on the overall market return for buyout fund of funds as determined by benchmark provider GHI. Individual vintage year benchmarks are the median SI-IRR for the applicable vintage years, at 31 December 2013.

SAMPLE 6   PRIVATE EQUITY: FUND OF FUNDS BY VINTAGE YEAR

Investments 2002 Fund of Funds Composite
Results Reported as of Calendar Year End

Calendar Year	Gross-of-Fees SI-IRR (%)	Net-of-Fees SI-IRR (%)	Benchmark SI-IRR (%)	Composite Assets ($ Mil)	Total Firm Assets ($ Mil)	# of Portfolios
2002*	2.5	−5.5	8.5	2.6	250	≤ 5
2003	−4.2	−12.3	−3.8	4.7	300	≤ 5
2004	12.5	6.5	14.4	7.5	350	≤ 5
2005	45.8	40.8	42.7	24.2	400	≤ 5
2006	35.6	31.5	30.2	21.6	450	≤ 5
2007	22.2	19.3	13.5	14.7	500	≤ 5
2008	17.4	15.5	8.1	11.8	550	≤ 5
2009	17.3	15.3	7.5	11.0	600	≤ 5
2010	16.5	14.8	8.0	9.3	650	≤ 5
2011	15.9	13.5	8.5	8.1	700	≤ 5
2012	16.8	14.0	10.3	6.5	750	≤ 5

*Returns are for the period from 1 May 2002 (inception date) through 31 December 2002.

Calendar Year	Cumulative Committed Capital ($ Mil)	Paid-In Capital ($ Mil)	Cumulative Distributions ($ Mil)	DPI	RVPI	TVPI	PIC
2002	20	3	0	0.00	1.04	1.04	0.15
2003	20	5	0	0.00	0.93	0.93	0.25
2004	20	8	2	0.22	0.94	1.16	0.40
2005	20	15	4	0.23	1.62	1.85	0.75
2006	20	17	12	0.71	1.25	1.96	0.85
2007	20	18	16	0.89	0.82	1.71	0.90
2008	20	19	17	0.89	0.62	1.51	0.95
2009	20	19	19	0.99	0.57	1.56	0.96
2010	20	20	23	1.18	0.47	1.65	0.98
2011	20	20	25	1.25	0.41	1.66	1.00
2012	20	20	29	1.45	0.33	1.78	1.00

Underlying Partnership Investments by Strategy
Results Reported as of 31 December 2012

Investment Strategy	SI-IRR Gross-of-Fees (%)	Benchmark Return (%)	Committed Capital ($ Mil)	Paid-In Capital ($ Mil)	Cumulative Distributions ($ Mil)	Assets ($ Mil)	DPI Multiple	RVPI Multiple	TVPI Multiple	PIC Multiple
Venture Capital	65.3	32.6	8.0	8.0	16.0	2.0	2.0	0.3	2.3	1.0
Buyout	11.3	10.2	12.0	12.0	13.0	4.5	1.1	0.4	1.5	1.0

Disclosures

Sample 6 Investments claims compliance with the Global Investment Performance Standards (GIPS®) and has prepared and presented this report in compliance with the GIPS standards. Sample 6 Investments has not been independently verified.

Sample 6 Investments is an independent private equity manager of fund of funds strategies with offices in Zurich, Menlo Park, New York, and Hong Kong. The composite was created in May 2002 and includes one closed-end fund that invests in buyout and venture capital funds. The fund of funds has an 8–10 year investment time horizon, but it may be longer based on the life of the underlying funds, which may be extended due to changes in investment and/or exit opportunities. As more fully described in the fund's offering memorandum, primary risks include industry and geographic concentration depending on investment opportunities, and liquidity risks due to the nature of the fund's investments.

The composite's vintage year is 2002, which was determined using the date of the initial capital call of the fund of funds. Returns are presented in US dollars.

The 2002 Fund of Funds Composite complies with PQR's valuation guidelines, which are consistent with the GIPS Valuation Principles. Valuations are normally based on valuations provided by the manager of the underlying investments' partnerships. Because fund investments are not publicly traded, all investments are considered to be valued using subjective unobservable inputs.

All returns for the 2002 Fund of Funds Composite reflect the deduction of administrative expenses (legal, auditing, etc.) of the closed-end fund. Gross returns do not reflect the deduction of Sample 6 Investments' management fees. Net returns reflect the deduction of actual management fees and accrued carried interest, if any.

The fund's SI-IRR calculation incorporates daily cash flows. Sample 6 Investments' annual management fee is 1% on the total committed capital.

The Vendor ABC Private Equity Fund of Funds Index (vintage year 2002) is used as the benchmark.

A complete list of the firm's composite descriptions is available upon request, as are policies for valuing portfolios, calculating performance, and preparing compliant presentations.

SAMPLE 7   PRIVATE EQUITY: PRIMARY FUND VEHICLE

**Private Equity Capital Management
2001 Venture Capital Composite
Results Reported as of 31 December**

Year End	Paid-In Capital (AUD Mil)	Since Inception Distributions (AUD Mil)	Cumulative Committed Capital (AUD Mil)	Composite Assets (AUD Mil)	% of Firm Assets
2001*	40.3	0.0	175.0	38.5	64.2
2002	82.3	1.0	175.0	78.8	52.5
2003	129.5	29.9	175.0	105.0	58.3
2004	143.5	42.3	175.0	120.8	41.6
2005	157.5	97.0	175.0	119.0	37.8
2006	166.2	129.3	175.0	112.0	31.1
2007	171.5	184.7	175.0	98.0	28.0
2008	182.5	184.7	175.0	78.8	21.0
2009	182.5	184.7	175.0	49.0	11.9
2010	182.5	184.7	175.0	31.5	7.5
2011	182.5	205.8	175.0	5.2	1.1

*Returns are for the period from 3 February 2001 (inception date) through 31 December 2001.

Year End	TVPI	DPI	RVPI	PIC	Composite Gross-of-Fees SI-IRR (%)	Composite Net-of-Fees SI-IRR (%)	Benchmark SI-IRR (%)
2001	0.96	0.00	0.96	0.23	−7.5	−9.5	−12.5
2002	0.97	0.01	0.96	0.47	0.3	−1.6	−3.5
2003	1.04	0.23	0.81	0.74	4.1	2.3	1.2
2004	1.14	0.29	0.84	0.82	8.2	6.4	7.4
2005	1.37	0.62	0.76	0.90	11.0	9.3	8.2
2006	1.45	0.78	0.67	0.95	13.0	10.1	9.7
2007	1.65	1.08	0.57	0.98	18.1	12.3	11.4
2008	1.44	1.01	0.43	1.04	16.9	10.4	10.1
2009	1.28	1.01	0.27	1.04	14.9	8.7	7.2

Year End	TVPI	DPI	RVPI	PIC	Composite Gross-of-Fees SI-IRR (%)	Composite Net-of-Fees SI-IRR (%)	Benchmark SI-IRR (%)
2010	1.18	1.01	0.17	1.04	14.0	7.7	6.8
2011	1.16	1.13	0.03	1.04	11.2	6.2	5.5

TVPI = Total Value to Since Inception Paid-In Capital
DPI = Since Inception Distributions to Since Inception Paid-In Capital
PIC = Since Inception Paid-In Capital to Cumulative Committed Capital
RVPI = Residual Value to Since Inception Paid-In Capital

Disclosures

Compliance Statement

Private Equity Capital Management claims compliance with the Global Investment Performance Standards (GIPS®) and has prepared and presented this report in compliance with the GIPS standards. Private Equity Capital Management has been independently verified for the periods 3 February 2001 through 31 December 2010.

Verification assesses whether (1) the firm has complied with all the composite construction requirements of the GIPS standards on a firm-wide basis and (2) the firm's policies and procedures are designed to calculate and present performance in compliance with the GIPS standards. The 2001 Venture Capital Composite has been examined for the periods 1 January 2005 through 31 December 2010. The verification and performance examination reports are available upon request.

Firm & Composite

Private Equity Capital Management ("PECM") is an independent private equity investment firm with offices in New York, London, and Sydney. The 2001 Venture Capital Composite includes one fund, whose objective is to seek long-term capital appreciation by acquiring minority interests in early-stage technology companies. The fund invests in technology companies in Europe, Asia Pacific, and emerging markets. European venture investments are more concentrated than in the other regions and are focused in a few high-quality companies. Exit opportunities include IPOs, trade sales, and secondary sales. Opportunities in China and India will be targeted for investment, and an allocation to Chinese high-tech will be at least 10% of the invested capital over the life of the fund. International venture capital investments are generally illiquid and are subject to currency risk. If investment opportunities and/or exit strategies become limited, the life of the fund may be extended and capital calls and distributions may be delayed. The 2001 Venture Capital Composite was created in 2001. The vintage year of the composite is 2001 and was determined by the year of the first drawdown. The firm's list of composite descriptions and the firm's policies for calculating performance and preparing compliant presentation are available upon request.

Input Data & Calculation

The 2001 Venture Capital Composite complies with the LMN Venture Capital Association's valuation guidelines as well as the GIPS Valuation Principles. Valuations are prepared by PECM's valuation committee and reviewed by an independent advisory board. All investments within the composite are valued using either a most recent transaction or an earnings multiple. Policies for valuing investments are available upon request. Due to the nature of private equity investments, all investments are valued using subjective unobservable inputs.

The SI-IRR calculation incorporates monthly cash flows for periods prior to 31 December 2009 and daily cash flows thereafter. Performance is expressed in Australian dollars (AUD).

Gross returns are net of transaction expenses and all administrative expenses. Net returns are net of transaction expenses, administrative expenses, management fees, and carried interest. The standard fee schedule currently in effect is as follows:

> The manager will receive an annual management fee equal to 2% of capital commitments. The manager's participation in profits (carried interest) begins after the limited partners have been provided an 8% preferred return. The manager collects 20% of the distributed profits from that point forward. Subsequently, if the amount of cumulative carried interest exceeds 20% of the net cumulative gains, the manager will repay the excess amount to the fund for distribution to the limited partners.

There is only one fund in the composite for all periods; therefore, the internal dispersion of portfolio returns is not applicable.

Benchmark

The benchmark return is derived from private equity dollar-weighted IRRs, and the calculation is based on the overall market return for international venture capital funds as published by Benchmark Provider GHI. Vintage year benchmarks are median returns for the applicable vintage year, as of each year end.

SAMPLE 8   INVESTMENTS LARGE-CAP SMA COMPOSITE

1 January 2001 through 31 December 2010

Year	Net Return (%)	XYZ Index Return (%)	Internal Dispersion (%)	As of 31 December			
				Number of Portfolios	Composite Assets ($ Millions)	Firm Assets ($ Millions)	% of SMA Portfolios
2010	8.4	10.2	0.7	1,834	2,125	18,222	100
2009	21.1	21.1	1.1	1,730	2,130	17,635	100
2008	−39.7	−39.8	1.0	1,631	2,141	19,246	100
2007	1.4	6.2	1.2	1,532	2,127	14,819	100
2006	11.4	10.5	0.9	1,428	2,116	12,362	100
2005	1.0	4.3	0.8	68	1,115	12,051	0
2004	6.8	4.9	1.0	52	1,110	13,419	0
2003	23.9	27.0	1.1	46	990	10,612	0
2002	−24.4	−19.1	0.9	38	975	9,422	0
2001	−17.7	−12.8	0.8	41	870	8,632	0

Notes:

1   Sample 8 Investments claims compliance with the Global Investment Performance Standards (GIPS®) and has prepared and presented this report in compliance with the GIPS standards. Sample 8 Investments has been independently verified for the period from 1 April 1996 through 31 December 2009.

Verification assesses whether (1) the firm has complied with all the composite construction requirements of the GIPS standards on a firm-wide basis and (2) the firm's policies and procedures are designed to calculate and present performance in compliance with the GIPS standards. The Large Cap SMA Composite has been examined for the period from 1 January 2006 through 31 December 2009. The verification and performance examination reports are available upon request.

2   Sample 8 Investments is an independent investment adviser registered under the Investment Advisers Act of 1940, was founded in March 1996, and manages global large-cap equity, fixed-income, and balanced strategies.

3   Beginning 1 January 2006, the composite includes only wrap fee (SMA) portfolios benchmarked to the XYZ Index. Performance results prior to 2006 are based on the Large-Cap Institutional Composite returns.

4   The Large-Cap SMA Composite is composed of portfolios invested in US equities which have a market capitalization greater than $5 billion.

5   The composite was created in February 2006. A list of composite descriptions is available upon request.

6   All returns are expressed in US dollars. Policies for valuing portfolios, calculating performance, and preparing compliant presentations are available upon request.

7 The XYZ Index returns are provided to represent the investment environment existing during the time periods shown. For comparison purposes, the index is fully invested and includes the reinvestment of income. The returns for the index do not include any trading costs, management fees, or other costs. Index returns have been taken from published sources.

8 "Pure" gross returns, presented below as supplemental information, from 2006 through 2010 do not reflect the deduction of any trading costs, fees, or expenses and are presented for comparison purposes only. "Pure" gross returns prior to 2006 reflect the deduction of trading costs. The SMA fee includes all charges for trading costs, portfolio management, custody, and other administrative fees. Net returns are calculated by subtracting the highest applicable SMA fee (2.50% on an annual basis, or 0.21% monthly) on a monthly basis from the "pure" gross composite monthly return. The standard fee schedule in effect is as follows: 2.50% on total assets.

9 The dispersion is measured by the equal-weighted standard deviation of annual returns of those portfolios that are included in the composite for the full year.

10 At 31 December 2010, the three-year annualized ex-post standard deviation of the composite and the benchmark are 12.3% and 13.2%, respectively.

11 Past performance is not an indicator of future results.

		Supplemental Information	
Year	"Pure" Gross Return* (%)	Net Return (%) Assuming 3% SMA Fees	Net Return (%) Assuming 2% SMA Fees
2010	11.1	7.9	9.0
2009	24.0	20.5	21.7
2008	−38.0	−40.1	−39.4
2007	4.0	0.9	2.0
2006	14.1	10.8	11.9
2005	3.5	0.5	1.5
2004	9.5	6.3	7.4
2003	26.9	23.3	24.5
2002	−22.3	−24.8	−23.9
2001	−15.5	−18.1	−17.2

* "Pure" gross-of-fees returns do not reflect the deduction of any expenses, including trading costs. "Pure" gross-of-fees returns are supplemental to net returns.

APPENDIX B: SAMPLE ADVERTISEMENTS

1.   SAMPLE ADVERTISEMENT WITHOUT PERFORMANCE

Generic Asset Management

Generic Asset Management is the institutional asset management division of Generic Inc. and is a registered investment advisory firm specializing in qualitative growth-oriented investment management.

Generic Asset Management claims compliance with the Global Investment Performance Standards (GIPS®). To receive a list of composite descriptions of Generic Asset Management and/or a presentation that complies with the GIPS standards, contact Jean Paul at (123) 456-7890, or write to Generic Asset Management, 123 Main Street, Returnsville 12345, or jpaul@genericassetmanagment.com.

2.   SAMPLE ADVERTISEMENT INCLUDING ONE-, THREE-, AND FIVE-YEAR ANNUALIZED RETURNS

Generic Asset Management: Global Equity Growth Composite			
	Ending 31 Mar 2012		
	1-Year	**3-Year Annualized**	**5-Year Annualized**
Global Equity Growth Composite	−0.3%	13.7%	0.1%
XYZ World Index	−0.5%	13.8%	−0.6%

Note: Returns are shown in US dollars net of fees.

Generic Asset Management is the institutional asset management subsidiary of Generic Inc. and is a registered investment adviser specializing in qualitative growth-oriented investment management. The Global Equity Growth strategy focuses on earnings, growth of earnings, and key valuation metrics. The benchmark is the XYZ World Index, which is designed to measure the equity market performance of developed market countries. The benchmark is market-cap weighted and is composed of all XYZ developed market indices.

Generic Asset Management claims compliance with the Global Investment Performance Standards (GIPS®). To receive a list of composite descriptions of Generic Asset Management and/or a presentation that complies with the GIPS standards, contact Jean Paul at (123) 456-7890, or write Generic Asset Management, One Plain Street, Returnsville 12345, or jpaul@genericassetmanagement.com.

3. SAMPLE ADVERTISEMENT INCLUDING PERIOD-TO-DATE AND ONE-, THREE-, AND FIVE-YEAR ANNUALIZED RETURNS

Generic Asset Management: Global Equity Growth Composite

	Ending 31 Mar 2012	Ending 31 Dec 2011		
	Period to Date (3 months)	1-Year	3-Year Annualized	5-Year Annualized
Global Equity Growth Composite	−3.84%	1.3%	15.0%	−1.2%
XYZ World Index	−4.94%	1.5%	14.1%	−0.7%

Note: Returns are shown in US dollars net of fees.

Generic Asset Management is the institutional asset management subsidiary of Generic Inc. and is a registered investment adviser specializing in qualitative growth-oriented investment management. The Global Equity Growth strategy focuses on earnings, growth of earnings, and key valuation metrics. The benchmark is the XYZ World Index, which is designed to measure the equity market performance of developed market countries. The benchmark is market-cap weighted and is composed of all XYZ developed market indices.

Generic Asset Management claims compliance with the Global Investment Performance Standards (GIPS®). To receive a list of composite descriptions of Generic Asset Management and/or a presentation that complies with the GIPS standards, contact Jean Paul at (123) 456-7890, or write Generic Asset Management, One Plain Street, Returnsville 12345, or jpaul@genericassetmanagement.com.

4. SAMPLE ADVERTISEMENT INCLUDING FIVE YEARS OF ANNUAL RETURNS

Generic Asset Management: Global Equity Growth Composite

	Period to Date (3 months to 31 Mar 2012)	Annual Returns Periods Ended 31 December				
		2011	2010	2009	2008	2007
Global Equity Growth Composite	−3.84%	1.3%	13.0%	33.0%	−40.6%	9.6%
XYZ World Index	−4.94%	1.5%	11.8%	30.8%	−40.3%	9.6%

Note: Returns are shown in US dollars net of fees.

Generic Asset Management is the institutional asset management subsidiary of Generic Inc. and is a registered investment adviser specializing in qualitative, growth-oriented investment management. The Global Equity Growth strategy focuses on earnings, growth of earnings, and key valuation metrics. The benchmark is the XYZ World Index, which is designed to measure the equity market performance of developed market countries. The benchmark is market-cap weighted and is composed of all XYZ developed market indices.

Generic Asset Management claims compliance with the Global Investment Performance Standards (GIPS®).
To receive a list of composite descriptions of Generic Asset Management and/or a presentation that complies with the GIPS standards, contact Jean Paul at (123) 456-7890, or write to Generic Asset Management, 123 Main Street, Returnsville 12345, or jpaul@genericassetmanagment.com.

APPENDIX C: SAMPLE LIST OF COMPOSITE DESCRIPTIONS

1   Unconstrained Activist UK Equity Composite

The Unconstrained Activist UK Equity Composite includes all institutional portfolios invested in both listed and unlisted UK equities that pursue an activist investment policy; there is no restriction on the market capitalization of companies held. Portfolios within this composite are highly concentrated, holding approximately 15 securities, so returns may have lower correlation with the benchmark than a fully diversified strategy. In times of increased market volatility, the composite characteristics may change significantly and stock liquidity could be reduced. Due to their more concentrated nature, portfolios will tend to have more stock-specific risk than a more diversified strategy. Portfolios can use both exchange-traded and OTC derivative contracts for efficient portfolio management, which may expose the strategy to counterparty risk. The benchmark is the FTSE All Share® Index.

2   Emerging Market High Yield Fixed Income Composite

The Emerging Market High Yield Fixed Income Composite includes all institutional and retail portfolios invested in high yield debt securities issued by countries outside the OECD. The strategy allows for investment in foreign currency denominated assets over which the manager has full discretion on hedging. The strategy aims to deliver a total return primarily through income but with some capital growth. High yield bonds carry increased levels of credit and default risk and are less liquid than government and investment grade bonds. Investment in less regulated markets carries increased political, economic, and issuer risk. The benchmark is the J.P. Morgan Emerging Market Bond Index (EMBI+).

3   UK Liquidity Plus Composite

The UK Liquidity Plus Composite includes all institutional portfolios invested in a broad range of short-dated interest-bearing deposits, cash equivalents, short-term commercial paper, and other money market investments issued by major UK clearing banks and lending institutions. The strategy has a targeted modified duration of less than one year. The principal investment objectives are preservation of capital, maintenance of liquidity, and provision of yield greater than that available for the benchmark, the three-month Libor rate. The UK Liquidity Plus strategy differs from more conventional cash strategies in that it additionally holds short-term commercial paper, which has a greater exposure to credit risk.

4   Socially Responsible Investment (SRI) Composite

The Socially Responsible Investment Composite includes all segregated institutional and pooled portfolios that invest in global equity securities issued by companies that make a positive contribution to society and the environment through sustainable and socially responsible practices. The strategy aims to provide long-term capital appreciation together with a growing income stream through investment in a portfolio of core equity holdings diversified by economic sector, industry group, and geographic business concentration. All foreign currency exposures are fully hedged back to US dollars.

The SRI process tends to screen out certain companies and sectors, which may result in a more concentrated strategy than a fully diversified strategy. Changes in legislation, scientific thinking, national and supra-national policies, and behaviors could significantly affect the stocks of companies held within the strategy. The benchmark is the Morningstar Ethical/SRI Global GIF Sector peer group.

5   Leveraged Bond Composite

The Leveraged Bond Composite includes all institutional segregated portfolios invested in a diversified range of high yield corporate and government bonds with the aim of providing investors with a high level of income while seeking to maximize the total return. The portfolios are invested in domestic and international fixed income securities of varying maturities. The strategy allows investment in exchange-traded and OTC derivative contracts (including, but not limited to, options, futures, swaps, and forward currency contracts) for the purposes of risk, volatility, and currency exposure management. The strategy allows leverage up to but not exceeding twice the value of a portfolio's investments through the use of repurchase financing arrangements with counterparties. Inherent in derivative instrument investments is the risk of counterparty default. Leverage may also magnify losses as well as gains to the extent that leverage is employed. The benchmark is the Barclays Capital Global Aggregate Bond Index.

6   Global Commodity Composite

The Global Commodity Composite includes institutional portfolios that globally invest in a diversified range of companies that provide exposure to commodities, energy, and materials. Investment is primarily through the common or ordinary stock of these companies. Investment directly in raw materials is allowable to a maximum exposure of 10%. Exchange-traded funds and exchange-traded commodity securities up to a maximum 20% exposure are also allowed. The base currency is US dollars, and any or all of the currency risk associated with investments in currencies other than dollars may be hedged between 0% and 100% at the manager's discretion. The strategy cannot gear or otherwise deploy leverage but may use exchange-traded derivative instruments for efficient portfolio management.

Investments directly or indirectly in commodities may add to portfolio volatility. Global commodity prices can be affected by changes in legislation, national and supra-national policies, and behaviors. In times of commodity price volatility, the liquidity of directly held commodities and the correlation with the broad market can change quickly. The benchmark is the Dow Jones–UBS Commodity Index Total Return^{SM}.

7   Large Cap Equity Growth Composite

The Large Cap Equity Growth Composite includes all institutional portfolios that invest in large capitalization US stocks that are considered to have growth in earnings prospects that is superior to that of the average company within the benchmark, the Russell 3000® Growth Index. The targeted tracking error between the composite and the benchmark is less than 3%.

8   Balanced Growth Composite

The Balanced Growth Composite includes all institutional balanced portfolios that invest in large-cap US equities and investment-grade bonds with the goal of providing long-term capital growth and steady income from a well-diversified strategy. Although the strategy allows for equity exposure ranging between 50% and 70%, the typical allocation is between 55% and 65%.

9   Currency Overlay Composite

The Currency Overlay Composite includes all institutional and retail portfolios invested in a broad range of foreign-currency-denominated deposits or instruments, such as forward contracts, futures, or foreign exchange derivatives. The principal investment objective is alpha generation through currency appreciation and/or risk mitigation from adverse movements in exchange rates where the original currency exposure stems from a global or international portfolio. Hedging strategies may range from passive to fully active. Currency-related investing carries inherent risks due to changes in macroeconomic policy, which can be amplified in the case of emerging markets, where political regime shifts and changes in the control of capital may be more prevalent. In volatile periods, liquidity and correlations between currencies may change expected returns drastically. Foreign exchange forwards and derivatives traded over the counter have counterparty default risk.

10   Asian Market Neutral Composite

The Asian Market Neutral Composite includes a single hedge fund with a market neutral strategy that invests in publically traded Asian equities with a market capitalization greater than $500 million. The strategy uses a risk controlled quantitative screening and optimization process that invests at least 85% of the net asset value in long equity positions and at least 85% of the net asset value in short equity positions. The long portion of the strategy will overweight those securities that have been quantitatively identified as potentially exhibiting superior and sustainable earnings growth compared with the market; conversely, the short portion of the strategy will consist of securities that have been identified as having inferior growth prospects or that may also be adversely affected by either specific events or by momentum considerations. The principal objective of the strategy is to outperform the return on three-month US Treasury Bills through active trading of long and short equity positions.

The Asian Market Neutral strategy seeks to dollar balance exposures between long and short positions so that broad market movements are neutralized. In certain market conditions, the investment process behind the strategy can give rise to unmatched country, sector, industry, market capitalization, and/or style bias exposures in the portfolio. The active trading strategy will involve significantly greater stock turnover when compared with passive strategies.

11   2001 Venture Capital Composite

The 2001 Venture Capital Composite includes one fund, whose objective is to seek long-term capital appreciation by acquiring minority interests in early-stage technology companies. The fund invests in technology companies in Europe, Asia Pacific, and emerging markets. European venture investments are more concentrated than in the other regions and are focused in a few high-quality companies. Exit opportunities include IPOs, trade sales, and secondary sales. Opportunities in China and India will be targeted for investment, and an allocation to Chinese high-tech will be at least 10% of the invested capital over the life of the fund. International venture capital investments are generally illiquid and are subject to currency risk. If investment opportunities and/or exit strategies become limited, the life of the fund may be extended and capital calls and distributions may be delayed.

12 2006 Buyout Strategy Fund of Funds Composite

The 2006 Buyout Strategy Fund of Funds Composite includes primary and secondary partnership investments with strategies focused on leveraged and growth-oriented buyouts primarily in the United States. Managers of partnerships are expected to focus on reducing costs, preparing companies for downturn, and providing operational improvement rather than financial engineering. Investments may be in small, medium, and large buyout partnerships, aiming to make selective commitments diversifying across stages, industries, and vintage years. Secondary deals take advantage of distressed primary partnership sales providing access to an increased mix of assets. The underlying funds are leveraged 100–300%. Private equity investments are illiquid and, therefore, if investment opportunities and/or exit strategies become limited, the life of the fund may be extended and capital calls and distributions may be delayed.

13 Value-Added Strategy Non-Closed-End Real Estate Composite

The Value-Added Strategy Composite consists of all discretionary open-end funds and separate accounts managed by the Firm using a value-added investment strategy with an equal income and appreciation focus and having a minimum portfolio size of $10 million. Portfolio management will invest in multi-family, office, industrial, and retail property types only within Asia that require correction or mitigation of the investments' operating, financial, redevelopment, and/or management risk(s). A moderate level of leverage ranging between 30% and 40% is used. Real estate investments are generally illiquid, and the investment outlook may change given the availability of credit or other financing sources.

14 Value-Added Strategy Closed-End Real Estate Composite

The Value-Added Strategy Composite includes a single closed-end commingled fund managed by the Firm using a value-added investment strategy with a focus on both income and appreciation. Portfolio management intends to invest in properties located in major markets within the United States with higher operational risk than traditional property types. The target level of leverage is 50% with a maximum allowable level of 60%. Real estate investments are generally illiquid, and the investment outlook may change given the availability of credit or other financing sources. If investment opportunities and/or exit strategies become limited, the life of the fund may be extended and capital calls and distributions may be delayed.

15 US Core Equity Composite (Terminated Composites)

The US Core Equity Composite includes all institutional portfolios and pooled funds managed to a GARP (growth at a reasonable price) strategy through investment in a high-quality, focused portfolio of domestic, large-capitalization stocks that are expected to generate returns above the S&P 500® Index over a market cycle. Sample Asset Management Firm uses a quantitative screening process together with fundamental research and then overlays macroeconomic factors and economic sector exposures to construct portfolios. The benchmark is the S&P 500 Index. Quantitative-driven investment screening relies on historical stock correlations, which can be adversely affected during periods of severe market volatility. The composite terminated in March 2009.

Detailed composite definitions are available upon request.